# REAL
# GOD
## IN THE
# REAL
# WORLD

**Published by**
**The Bible Reading Fellowship**
15 The Chambers, Vineyard
Abingdon OX14 3FE
United Kingdom
Tel: +44 (0)1865 319700
Email: enquiries@brf.org.uk
Website: www.brf.org.uk

ISBN 978 0 85746 265 7

First published 2013

10 9 8 7 6 5 4 3 2 1 0

**Acknowledgments**
Unless otherwise indicated, scripture quotations are taken from The Holy Bible, New
International Version (Anglicised edition). Copyright © 1979, 1984, 2011 by Biblica (formerly
International Bible Society). Used by permission of Hodder & Stoughton Publishers, an
Hachette UK company. All rights reserved. 'NIV' is a registered trademark of Biblica (formerly
International Bible Society). UK trademark number 1448790.

The paper used in the production of this publication was supplied by mills that source their
raw materials from sustainably managed forests. Soy-based inks were used in its printing and
the laminate film is biodegradable.

A catalogue record for this book is available from the British Library

Printed in Singapore by Craft Print International Ltd

# REAL
# GOD
## IN THE
# REAL
# WORLD

Advent and Christmas
readings on the coming
of Christ

Trystan
Owain Hughes

## Acknowledgments

*Thank you to my friends and family who have supported my writing down the years, and to all who have written kind emails, Facebook and Twitter messages, and letters of support after reading my books. Your enthusiasm, love and support have made the process of writing even more worthwhile.*

*A special thank you to: Kath and Mike Lawley (for ensuring I didn't have to face Christmases alone during my curacy); my dad, Gwilym Berw (for help in translation); Stacey Baldwin (for allowing me to let the world know about her love of trees); Paul Francis (for his support and wise counsel); and Lukas Lacey-Hughes (for the advice about the films I refer to in this book). Thanks also to the following for advice and assistance: Tony Campolo, Michele Browne, Christopher Frost, Gareth and Pamela Harcombe, Sally Humble-Jackson, Nicola Davies, James Karran, Janice Brown, Devi Prasanna, Delyth Liddell, David Lumley and Perry Buck.*

*Thank you to Archbishop Barry Morgan and Bishop David Wilbourne for supporting my ministry.*

*Thank you to everyone at BRF, especially Naomi Starkey* (diolch!), *for believing others would find my thoughts and reflections worthwhile reading.*

*Thank you to my family in North Wales (especially to my Mum, Ros, and Dad, Berw) for being happy for me to include stories of my childhood.*

*Finally, a big* danke schön *to my wonderful family—to Lukas and Lena for bringing so much fun and laughter into my life, and especially to my beautiful and talented wife, Sandra, for her love, encouragement and many wise suggestions after faithfully and diligently reading every chapter.*

# Contents

Introduction ....................................................................6

1–7 December: The Word made flesh...............................9

8–14 December: Christ in our neighbour .........................37

15–21 December: Christ in the natural world..................65

22–28 December: Christ in our lives ...............................92

29 December–4 January: Being Christ in the world .......118

5–6 January: Putting our hand in his hand ....................144

Using this book with a group .........................................152

# Introduction

*God came to us, a man creating creatures.*
*He was God and man,*
*and was equally gifted as God and man.*
*A small, large giant; a powerful, weak Son;*
*his cheeks were pale.*
*Wealthy and poor, our Father and Brother,*
*Maker of Brothers.*
*Jesus is the one whom we welcome as King of Kings;*
*Lofty and lowly Emmanuel;*
*Honey for our thoughts.*

'A SON WAS GIVEN' ('*MAB A'N RHODDED*') BY
MADOG AP GWALLTER (C. 1250).
TRANSLATED BY GWILYM BERW HUGHES AND TRYSTAN OWAIN HUGHES

Christmas time certainly means different things to different
people. Alongside the religious and spiritual element, a recent
online poll showed that we each look forward to different
aspects of the festive season—time with family, giving gifts,
the food and drink, catching up with old friends, watching
children opening their presents, Christmas TV and so on.
In my own family when I was growing up, we would have
added board games to that list. My very favourite board game
was Monopoly. I'm from a large family—I have three brothers
and one sister—and, I have to say, our games at home used
to get a bit too serious. The one thing that was essential to
remember was that you never, ever, *ever* left the table to go
to the toilet. By the time you got back, your cash would
have been stolen, your hotels would have moved, and you

would have been mysteriously banished to jail! These days it is a bit harder to cheat in Monopoly, as some of the latest editions of the game do not have pretend money. Instead, they have small credit cards and little swipe machines that clock up how much money you have—so Monopoly theft is becoming a thing of the past. But now the problem is that Monopoly fraud is rampant in houses up and down the country at Christmas time!

Games certainly need rules, otherwise they descend into chaos. In fact, life itself is subject to fundamental laws. Without the law of gravity, we would all be floating around aimlessly. Without the laws of nature, our farmers would struggle to grow our food. Without the laws of the land, it would not be safe to leave our houses. Without the Highway Code, there would be carnage on our roads. It is easy, therefore, for us to fall into the trap of thinking that everything in life is about rules and regulations. Our faith, however, is not a religion of rules and laws. From his own experience of first-century Israelite culture, Jesus himself recognised that laws can be taken to extremes and so become unhelpful and burdensome. This is as true today as it was 2,000 years ago. There was once a festive report in British newspapers about a little donkey in Mexico who was incarcerated for biting a man. This was no special animal prison, though: the donkey was quite literally put in jail, alongside human prisoners. *The Daily Telegraph* interviewed the local police officer, who announced that they were only sticking to the rules, and the donkey had, after all, broken the law. 'Around here, if someone commits a crime they are jailed,' he said, 'no matter who they are.' The situation may seem rather farcical, but at least it gave British tabloids the opportunity to come up with some great headlines: 'The

Law is an Ass', 'Donkey Jailed for Ass-ault' and my absolute favourite, 'Police Play Pin the Bail on the Donkey'!

Rules and laws certainly serve a purpose, but they can also become a burden to us, especially when they are taken too far and become legalistic. The New Testament takes us away from a faith which was rooted in strict laws, and introduces us to a faith which is centred on a person—a person who came to show how much we are loved, to transform our characters, and to bring light into our darkness. That person is Jesus himself. At Christmas time we are reminded that 'God came to us, a man creating creatures,' as Madog ap Gwallter put it. After all, we are constantly told by our churches that the 'real meaning' of Christmas is Jesus himself. So perhaps the online poll's list of our favourite aspects of the season should take a firm backseat to the story of the birth of our Saviour. However, as we work through this book, I hope you will find that we need to be wary of such a rigid separation of our religious and secular lives. Yes, Jesus is definitely the 'real meaning' of Christmas, and we should certainly affirm that fact. But that very recognition should then inspire us to discover him not only in any church service that we may attend on Christmas morning, but also in every other part of our Christmas experience—in the sumptuous food and drink that we enjoy; in the gifts that we give and receive; in the sparkling tinsel and the beautiful trees; in the Christmas songs playing on our radios; in the films that we watch on our TVs; in the frost on our windscreens and the snow scenes that adorn our Christmas cards; and in the wonderful company of our family and friends who join us to celebrate the birth of the Saviour.

# 1–7 December

# The Word made flesh

When comedian Ricky Gervais was interviewed about his childhood on an episode of the talk-show *Inside the Actor's Studio* (first broadcast in the USA in 2009), he recalled his attendance at his local Sunday school between the ages of four and eight. These days, Gervais is one of the UK's most vocal atheists, and he regularly discusses publically his distaste of faith, including once debating with the then Archbishop of Canterbury, Rowan Williams, on Simon Mayo's Radio 5 show. In nostalgically recalling his childhood days, however, he admitted that he held a deep fascination with the figure of Jesus and with his radical teachings. 'I thought he was amazing,' he told the TV interviewer, 'just a brilliant guy.' It was Christ's compassion, kindness and courage which particularly drew Gervais to this lowly carpenter from first-century Palestine. 'I loved Jesus,' he asserted as he enthused about Christ's humanity. Yet, for Gervais, God himself was a distant, magical figure whom he rejected outright.

It is refreshing to hear such a prominent atheist speak about Jesus in such a positive manner. However, the Christmas story teaches us that Gervais's assertions that 'God was magic' and 'Jesus was just a man' are very much mistaken. The central message of the Christmas narrative is the incarnation—that the baby Jesus is God 'made flesh'. In the words of the carol 'Hark! the herald Angels sing': 'Veiled in flesh the Godhead see, / Hail the incarnate Deity!' In other words, Christmas introduces us to the idea that God knows exactly what it's like to be a human, and so he should never again be considered by us as simply supernatural magic. Rather, he is 'a small, large giant; a powerful, weak Son… lofty *and* lowly', as Madog ap Gwallter put it.

The traditional lessons and carols service at Christmas usually ends with the prologue from John's Gospel: 'The Word became flesh and made his dwelling among us. We have seen his glory, the glory of the one and only Son, who came from the Father, full of grace and truth' (John 1:14). There is a reason why this passage appears right at the beginning of John's Gospel. After all, it captures the whole purpose of Christ's birth, life, death and resurrection—that God became flesh in order to show us that we are not as far from him as we might think. In fact, we can connect with him at any time, as his incarnation continues today in the expreiences of our everyday lives: Jesus comes to us through the people we meet, the conversations we have and the places we visit. When we open our eyes and recognise that the Word made flesh is still in our world, the Word will be made fresh in our lives!

# 1 December

# The journey

## Matthew 2:13–15

When they had gone, an angel of the Lord appeared to Joseph in a dream. 'Get up,' he said, 'take the child and his mother and escape to Egypt. Stay there until I tell you, for Herod is going to search for the child to kill him.'

So he got up, took the child and his mother during the night and left for Egypt, where he stayed until the death of Herod. And so was fulfilled what the Lord had said through the prophet: 'Out of Egypt I called my son.'

It dawned on me recently how many stories in the Bible involve travelling. At the beginning of the Old Testament, Adam and Eve are thrown out of Eden to wander the world, and from then on everybody seems to be on a journey. The Israelites, for example, start off as a wandering, nomadic people in Genesis, and (apart from a settled period during the time of the kings) appear to travel almost continually throughout the Old Testament. In the story of the exodus, Moses leads God's people out of Egypt; the story of the exile describes them being taken to Babylon and returning again. Individuals also embark on all sorts of journeys: Noah floats around in his big ark; Joseph gets taken to Egypt; Jonah is thrown from a boat and gets swallowed by a big fish; and so on. In the New Testament, the journeys continue, not least in the Christmas narratives, with Mary's trip to her cousin

Elizabeth; the journey to Bethlehem; the wise men following the star; and the escape to Egypt.

All this travelling is not so unusual. Many of us regularly embark on journeys, whether they are long or short, arduous or fun, or for work or pleasure. Furthermore, even our lives are like journeys, and these journeys, like those of the disciples on the road to Emmaus and the apostle Paul on the road to Damascus, can be transformed in an amazing way if we recognise that Christ is travelling alongside us.

To appreciate the presence of God in our lives in this way, we have to accept that journeys are not only about getting somewhere. A few weeks ago I bought my first Ordnance Survey map, and bravely went exploring my local countryside on a wet Sunday afternoon. I was amazed what I discovered with my map—forests, lakes, disused mines, ruined castles, picnic sites and so on. A road atlas or a Sat Nav would not have shown me any of these things—their job would simply have been to get me from A to B, while everything in between those two points would have mattered very little. Many of us would have to admit that we approach most of our journeys like this, as we obsess about the destination and ignore or relegate the beauty of the journey itself—the countryside, the wildlife, the beautiful villages, the music playing on our radios and the conversations with those travelling with us.

By contrast, when people travelled in the past, the journey itself was often as important as the destination. To the pilgrims in Geoffrey Chaucer's 14th-century book *The Canterbury Tales*, for example, the endpoint was secondary to the stories they told each other as they travelled. After all 'Tales' is the operative word in the title, not the beautiful city at which Chaucer does not even record them arriving. I had a similar experience myself when, as a six-year-old, my family travelled down from North Wales to Cardiff on a special train that had been organised for rugby supporters. We were not ourselves going to the rugby, but were simply having a day out in our capital city. In fact, I can't remember what we actually did in Cardiff that day, but I do remember the journey as if it were yesterday—the stories the old rugby fans told, the jokes that shocked my mum, and the rules of poker that the fans taught my innocent little six-year-old self! Too frequently in today's hectic world we jump into our cars and go into 'auto-pilot' until we arrive at our destination. We can travel many miles without noticing anything about the world around us unless it might affect our arrival time.

If we live our lives like road atlases or Sat Navs, regarding life as a series of journeys from A to B, then we will miss truly experiencing life. Whatever our achievement-based society tries to tell us, life is not about getting somewhere. Rather, life should be about finding glimpses of the Christ child in our everyday travels. The Christmas narratives may indeed start with a number of journeys, but we should not forget that the story did not finish in Bethlehem or after the journey to Egypt. It did not even finish on the cross at Calvary. The journey continues everyday as we meet with Jesus and live lives centred on experiencing him and sharing his love. After all, the kingdom of God is not merely a future hope; it can be found this very moment, in the midst of all our journeys. Paul, on his own missionary travels, would remind his listeners that Christ was to be found among them. Our job is to enter his kingdom each day by recognising his wonderful fingerprints in our everyday lives—in nature, in laughter, in kindness, in love, in children, in art, in music, in family, in friends, in food, in sunshine and in somebody's smile.

## Reflection

*Think of a journey you have made in the past. It may have been abroad or in your own country. Take some time to recall the actual details of travelling there and back. What did you see? Who did you talk to? Life is about recognising Christ in all our journeys. Take time to look out for him today, wherever you go (near or far) and in whatever ways he comes to you. Whatever you do during the day, open your eyes to his presence, open your ears to his call and open your heart to his love, and then thank him for the blessings in your life.*

# 2 December

# Christ as our cornerstone

### Ephesians 2:19–22

You are no longer foreigners and strangers, but fellow citizens with God's people and also members of his household, built on the foundation of the apostles and prophets, with Christ Jesus himself as the chief cornerstone. In him the whole building is joined together and rises to become a holy temple in the Lord. And in him you too are being built together to become a dwelling in which God lives by his Spirit.

I was born and brought up in a small town on the coast of North Wales called Penmaenmawr. As I've already mentioned, I am one in a family of five children, and when we kids played in our garden on the occasional sunny day we had in North Wales, we each used to choose an action-hero character to play. One of my brothers was the Incredible Hulk, another was Luke Skywalker, and my sister was always Wonder Woman. As for me, well I always used to choose the 19th-century Prime Minister, William Ewart Gladstone! This might make you think that I was an unpopular, pretentious child. But think again… Gladstone was a superstar in our small village. Penmaenmawr had been his favourite holiday destination, and we've never forgotten his wonderful patronage. We have a monument to him in the town square, we continually complain that our present Prime Minister 'is not as good as Gladstone', and Penmaenmawr's Anglican church, St Seiriol's, is inscribed with his name. I can even just about remember what it says:

'On 20th August 1867 Mrs Catherine Glynne Gladstone, the wife of the Prime Minster William E. Gladstone, laid the cornerstone of this church.'

Many 19th-century churches have similar plaques, to commemorate the laying of the cornerstone by some famous figure. It was the Victorian equivalent of the scissor-wielding celebrities who cut through red ribbon to celebrate the opening of a new shopping centre or sports hall today. But the importance of the cornerstone shouldn't be underestimated. Ask any architect, and they will tell you that the cornerstone is the very first stone set in the construction of a building. It is used to make sure the other stones are placed in the correct position. If the cornerstone is poorly positioned, the likelihood is that the whole building will either look ridiculous or, worse still, just collapse. In the Ancient Near East, the ceremony of laying the cornerstone involved all sorts of different rituals. Some cultures placed offerings of grain, wine and oil under the stone; others placed animal sacrifices. But if you think that's strange, in ancient Japan beautiful maidens were buried alive under the cornerstone, as a prayer to defend buildings against disaster. Medieval Christians were less harsh on their beautiful maidens, and so they opted to place relics of saints under the stone.

Our passage today, from Paul's letter to the Ephesians, refers to Jesus as the 'chief cornerstone' of the Church. The fact that our churches are actual buildings, and that Paul goes on to describe a holy temple, can serve to mask the importance of this metaphor. After all, we must remember that, in his letters, Paul does not refer to 'the Church' (*ekklesia*) as a building or as an institution. Rather, as this passage intimates, he is actually referring to a community, whom he calls 'God's people'. Jesus, therefore, should be the cornerstone of each of our lives! The theologian Dorothee Soelle wrote a wonderful alternative creed in which she warns us from burying Jesus in our church buildings. In this creed, she expresses her fear that Jesus 'died in vain', because we entombed him in our places of worship and thus 'betrayed his revolution'.

All of us certainly need to build our lives on something. These days, many people choose the desire to succeed, or the pursuit of material wealth, or the need to be loved. As Christians, we choose the figure of Jesus himself, so all our desires and needs should be in reference to this cornerstone, on and around which we build our lives, and without which our lives would collapse. We should not, then, be hiding Christ in the services and traditions of our churches, where he becomes a beautiful Japanese maiden buried underneath our cornerstone, or just a name printed on that stone. Rather, we should allow the living Christ actually to *be* the cornerstone itself, underpinning the way we think, the way we act and the way we live.

Our daily task should, in the light of this, be to ensure that we each make Christ our own personal cornerstone, and actively show to those around us what that means—by showing love, compassion and concern for everyone we meet. A friend of mine has 'the Word became flesh' tattooed on his arm in Greek, but we obviously don't need to be rushing out to get tattoos to show the centrality of Jesus in our lives! Just as Penmaenmawr's church has its cornerstone marked with the name of a former Prime Minister, so we should be showing through our daily lives exactly who our cornerstone is, so it is clear to all who come into contact with us.

## Reflection

*Think about how you have shown that Christ is your cornerstone this past week. It may have been through giving time to someone in need, or caring for his creation, or simply talking to people about the difference he makes in your life. Ask God to give you more opportunities to show others the importance of your relationship with Jesus. Remember, though, that such opportunities should never be self-glorifying or make us feel proud or superior. Reflect on the following verse: 'Let your light shine before others, that they may see your good deeds and glorify your Father in heaven' (Matthew 5:16).*

# Who is Christ?

### Matthew 16:13–19

When Jesus came to the region of Caesarea Philippi, he asked his disciples, 'Who do people say the Son of Man is?'

They replied, 'Some say John the Baptist; others say Elijah; and still others, Jeremiah or one of the prophets.'

'But what about you?' he asked. 'Who do you say I am?'

Simon Peter answered, 'You are the Messiah, the Son of the living God.'

Jesus replied, 'Blessed are you, Simon son of Jonah, for this was not revealed to you by flesh and blood, but by my Father in heaven. And I tell you that you are Peter, and on this rock I will build my church, and the gates of Hades will not overcome it. I will give you the keys of the kingdom of heaven; whatever you bind on earth will be bound in heaven, and whatever you loose on earth will be loosed in heaven.'

A friend of mine always used to tell me, 'You only hear what you want to hear.' Certainly for many years I was totally confused as to why The Beatles sang about frying chickens and baby donkeys. It turns out the lyrics to the song are 'She's got a ticket to ride' and 'My baby don't care' rather than 'She's got a chicken to fry' and 'My baby donkey'! But psychologists tell us that I am not alone in my tendency to mishear certain things. Recent research has even demonstrated that we humans really do suffer from what they describe as 'selective hearing'. It might come as no surprise to you that men are especially prone to this affliction. 'Oh yes,' a woman told an interviewer in a recent news report, 'my husband has that: he answers me when I ask him what he wants for tea, but doesn't hear me when I ask him to do the dishes.' People do indeed only hear what they want to hear!

In reality, we're selective in many things in our lives, not just our hearing. Christmas is a time when many will start to explore the question of who Jesus actually was. In our passage today, we see this was happening even during Jesus' ministry. 'Who do people say the Son of Man is?' asks Jesus. And the disciples answer, 'Some say John the Baptist; others say Elijah; and still others, Jeremiah or one of the prophets.' This divergence of views about who Jesus was has continued right down to today. Everyone, whether Christian or not, seems to have their own view about Jesus, and this not only reflects what they read from the Bible, but also their own background, their own culture, and their own personality. We only have to look at different countries around the world to find this: Indian churches display pictures of an Indian Jesus; the Chinese have a Chinese Jesus; Africans have a black Jesus; and, in the past at least, the British have had a peculiarly Western Jesus, with many churches' stained-glass windows showing a tall, blonde figure! In the Middle Ages, the English even used to taunt the French before war by shouting, 'The Pope may be French, but Jesus Christ is English!'

The poet William Blake recognised that our views of Jesus are naturally influenced by our backgrounds, whether that is through our culture or via what we are taught in church:

*The vision of Christ that thou dost see*
*Is my vision's greatest enemy.*
*Thine has a great hook nose like thine;*
*Mine has a snub nose like to mine…*
*Both read the Bible day and night,*
*But thou read'st black where I read white.*

FROM 'THE EVERLASTING GOSPEL' BY WILLIAM BLAKE (1757–1827)

It is quite natural for us to view some details about Jesus from our own perspective. We are influenced by how our particular church traditions and cultures teach us to read the Bible. We must learn to respect, and be willing to engage with, the pictures of Jesus that other people have, even when they differ somewhat from ours. When we do, we might be surprised that they can teach us something about Jesus that we had not previously noticed. In a sense, we are all looking at the chief cornerstone from different sides and, by opening our eyes and our hearts, we can learn so much from asking about the view from the other sides!

There is one thing, however, that all Christians, whatever their backgrounds, can agree on—that God's Son truly reflects the Father. In other words, the small child in a manger came to teach us how to love, to give us joy and peace in our hearts, and, in his eventual death and resurrection, to break through our suffering and bring us hope. As such, whatever the details of how we personally view Jesus, we can stand alongside Peter in asserting that 'You are the Messiah, the Son of the living God.'

## Reflection

*Imagine you are given 50 million pounds to make a film about Jesus. You have no script except the Gospel texts and your film will only be an hour and a half long. What kind of Jesus would you present? Think about and reflect upon your picture of Jesus. How does he look? What does he do? What kinds of things does he say? Ask someone else about how they view Jesus. How does that differ from your film's picture? What can you learn from their picture?*

# Christ the King

**Matthew 21:1–11**

As they approached Jerusalem and came to Bethphage on the Mount of Olives, Jesus sent two disciples, saying to them, 'Go to the village ahead of you, and at once you will find a donkey tied there, with her colt by her. Untie them and bring them to me. If anyone says anything to you, say that the Lord needs them, and he will send them right away.'

This took place to fulfil what was spoken through the prophet:

*'Say to Daughter Zion,*
*"See, your king comes to you,*
*gentle and riding on a donkey,*
*and on a colt, the foal of a donkey."'*

The disciples went and did as Jesus had instructed them. They brought the donkey and the colt and placed their cloaks on them for Jesus to sit on. A very large crowd spread their cloaks on the road, while others cut branches from the trees and spread them on the road. The crowds that went ahead of him and those that followed shouted,

*'Hosanna to the Son of David!'*
*'Blessed is he who comes in the name of the Lord!'*
*'Hosanna in the highest heaven!'*

When Jesus entered Jerusalem, the whole city was stirred and asked, 'Who is this?'

The crowds answered, 'This is Jesus, the prophet from Nazareth in Galilee.'

When I was a child, growing up in the wilds of Snowdonia before the days of computers, Sky TV and the Nintendo Wii™, my brother and I used to delight in the simplest of little games. One of our favourites was to find anything that was high—a tree, a hill, a ladder, a table—and then to fight each other, quite literally, to see who could get to the top first. As you can probably imagine, it was not the most popular game with my parents, and I remember many an unhappy afternoon in A&E! If either of us did reach the top without serious injury, we won the prestigious right to say the little rhyme, 'I'm the king of the castle, you're the dirty rascal.'

This rhyme teaches us that being a king is a good thing, and being a dirty rascal is, well, not so good! Many of us would jump at the chance to be king or queen for a day. We'd naturally think we were being offered the prospect of unlimited wealth, power and authority. Not one of us would be so excited if the glamorous carriage we were offered was a stubborn donkey, our precious crown was made of the sharpest thorns, our clothes were stripped from us, and then, finally, we were nailed to our throne.

People in first-century Palestine would have had similar ideas to us about what constituted a king—a rich, powerful political ruler. By that time, the Jews were expecting such a king to save them from Roman rule. They looked to the Old Testament prophecies and to the expectation that a new King David would come to free them from oppression. The film *King of Kings* (1961) presents Judas Iscariot as someone who was desperate for Jesus to become such a powerful ruler—the king of kings. He hands Jesus over to the Romans in the hope that this will force him to react and start a bloody revolution that will lead to him capturing political power. This idea of Judas as someone who misunderstands and misinterprets the kind of kingship Jesus desires, rather than as someone who is treacherous or greedy for money, is known as the DeQuincey Theory, after its first proponent in the English-speaking world, Thomas DeQuincey (1785–1859).

Yet, right at the beginning of his ministry, Christ had already rejected worldly power when tempted by it in the wilderness. Wealth and power do not hold any significance in Jesus' kingdom. They merely bring short-lived happiness, and will leave us greedy for more. If we make such things rule our thoughts and actions, we become the 'dirty rascals'. We should instead be looking towards Jesus' servant kingship as a model for our lives and relationships. By doing this we show our non-Christian neighbours that our faith is about following Christ's example of love, compassion and peace. We should be demonstrating to our world a selfless love which counters the desire for wealth and success that has become so prominent in today's world. When we do this, we too choose a donkey over a horse and become servant kings and queens ourselves.

## Reflection
*Someone once said that the word love could be spelled 't-i-m-e'. Consider how often you lay aside things that keep your life hectic and just spend time with people. Part of servanthood is simply being there for people. So this week take time out of your busy schedule to stop and talk with the people you meet, especially if they are people you wouldn't normally talk to.*

# Jesus is coming

## Isaiah 40:3–11

*A voice of one calling:*
*'In the wilderness prepare*
*   the way for the Lord;*
*make straight in the desert*
*   a highway for our God.*
*Every valley shall be raised up,*
*   every mountain and hill made low;*
*the rough ground shall become level,*
*   the rugged places a plain.*
*And the glory of the Lord will be revealed,*
*   and all people will see it together.*
*      For the mouth of the Lord has spoken.'*

*A voice says, 'Cry out.'*
*   And I said, 'What shall I cry?'*

*'All people are like grass,*
*   and all their faithfulness is like the flowers of the field.*
*The grass withers and the flowers fall,*
*   because the breath of the Lord blows on them.*
*   Surely the people are grass.*
*The grass withers and the flowers fall,*
*   but the word of our God endures for ever.'*

*You who bring good news to Zion,*
*   go up on a high mountain.*

*You who bring good news to Jerusalem,*
  *lift up your voice with a shout,*
*lift it up, do not be afraid;*
  *say to the towns of Judah,*
  *'Here is your God!'*
*See, the Sovereign Lord comes with power,*
  *and he rules with a mighty arm.*
*See, his reward is with him,*
  *and his recompense accompanies him.*
*He tends his flock like a shepherd:*
  *he gathers the lambs in his arms*
*and carries them close to his heart;*
  *he gently leads those that have young.*

A number of years back, newspapers reported that a young Brazilian nurse, who was working in Stockholm, Sweden, had been asked by the hospital authorities to change his name, after concerns that it might cause confusion among patients. His name was Jesus Manuel and his superiors had become concerned that their patients might get the wrong idea if they were told that 'Jesus is coming soon.' The young nurse, who was asked to use his second name alone, was quite reasonable about the whole situation. 'If they thought that Jesus was coming,' he told the local press, 'they might believe that they were already dead!'

The phrase 'Jesus is coming' has certainly come to signify quite a negative thing. For some people it is seen as relating to death, while for others, it is associated with the end of time and with the idea that Jesus is to come back to earth to judge humankind. 'Jesus is coming' has even become a joke to many outside the Church. I remember that one of the most popular T-shirts when I was studying in Oxford had the slogan 'Jesus is coming, so look busy'!

Our passage today from Isaiah was later used by John the Baptist to announce the commencement of Jesus' ministry, and it paints a very positive picture of the coming of the servant king. In the ancient world, before a king made a journey to another country, roads were built or improved so that he could travel in comfort. By using this Isaiah quote, John the Baptist was suggesting that people had to make way for a new king in their hearts—a king who can, if we let him, bring wonderfully liberating changes to our lives.

William Holman Hunt's painting *The Light of the World* (1853) shows a crowned Jesus holding a lantern and knocking on a door. The door represents the door to our hearts, but it has no handle on the outside, only weeds and overgrown brambles. In other words, we personally have to open the door to Jesus from the inside and welcome the king into our hearts. Once we do that, the wonderful thing is that he then helps us to clear away the weeds around our heart that have accumulated down the years. In doing this, Christ changes our lives in so many ways, not least by freeing us from the negative or oppressive thoughts that keep many of us in chains. The film *The Shawshank Redemption* (1994) is set in a prison. The main character persuades his fellow inmates that freedom can be found inside the walls, as it is rooted in our minds. 'There's something inside that they can't get to,' he tells them, 'something inside that they can't touch.' By making Christ the king in our hearts, our minds are no longer behind the iron bars of a prison. Rather, we are free to accept the hope, peace and love that Christ brings.

Hearing that 'Jesus is coming', then, should not be regarded as scary or negative—and it is certainly not something that merely happens at the end of time. Rather, Jesus is coming to us right now, and accepting him is not simply a decision to be made once, but one we make every single day. As such, we have to ensure that the bolt on the door of our hearts is unlocked and that we allow Jesus to tend our heart's garden continually. By doing so, the path is always prepared for our king to bring us daily his wonderful freedom for our hearts and minds.

## Reflection

*Think of Holman Hunt's painting* The Light of the World. *If possible, look it up on the internet, or in a book at your local library. What are the weeds and brambles in your life? They might be worry, anxiety, vanity, money, the desire for success, or anything else that gets in the way of your relationship with God. Thank Jesus that he helps you clear those weeds and frees your heart and mind. If you have found a picture of* The Light of the World, *take some time to reflect on it. How does it speak to you?*

# Peace on earth and goodwill to all

## Luke 2:8–14

There were shepherds living out in the fields nearby, keeping watch over their flocks at night. An angel of the Lord appeared to them, and the glory of the Lord shone around them, and they were terrified. But the angel said to them, 'Do not be afraid. I bring you good news that will cause great joy for all the people. Today in the town of David a Saviour has been born to you; he is the Messiah, the Lord. This will be a sign to you: you will find a baby wrapped in cloths and lying in a manger.'

Suddenly a great company of the heavenly host appeared with the angel, praising God and saying,

> 'Glory to God in the highest heaven,
>   and on earth peace to those on whom his favour rests.'

I recently watched a documentary about the soldiers in the World War I trenches, playing football on Christmas Day. It was Christmas morning, 1914, and already the horror of the war was becoming clear. Many had already lost their lives, and the soldiers were cold, deflated and hungry. Suddenly, a shout was heard from the German trench: '*Fröhliche Weihnachten*! Merry Christmas!' After a brief silence, one of the British soldiers replied, 'Merry Christmas to you too!' It was then that one German soldier took a huge risk: he put his gun down, climbed out of his trench, and walked over to British guns pointing at him. 'I wanted to wish you a merry Christmas in person,' he said in good English to the startled British soldiers. Within an hour, a 24-hour truce had been declared up and down the trenches. The soldiers gave gifts to their enemies, showed photos of their families to them, laughed with them, and shared precious food with them. The next day, the soldiers went back to killing each other. But just for 24 hours, Christmas, and all that Christ's incarnation means, had conquered hatred. Even in the darkness and pain of war, the hope, joy, love and peace of Christmas time shone through.

I remember the time when it suddenly dawned on me quite how important the message of Christmas is. It was 1979 and once again I was eagerly waiting to see which character I would play in the school's nativity play. I never got the best roles, but this year was to be particularly bad. I remember it was announced who was going to be Mary and Joseph, and I wasn't Joseph. Then they announced the kings and the shepherds, but my name was still conspicuously absent. Then an awful realisation came over me—there were only the angels to go! My heart was in my mouth as they announced the angels one by one, and I breathed a sigh of relief when my name was not mentioned. Then, finally, I heard my name. 'Trystan,' the teacher said, 'you've got a very important role—you're going to be a... tree.' Unfortunately, this was no special talking tree, or even a sparkling Christmas tree. I was simply an ordinary tree, standing with my hands out, behind the stable, saying nothing. I remember that rather boring role well, though, because it gave me a chance just to stand and listen to the others who were acting. And I remember the sense of awe and amazement when I heard the words 'peace on earth and goodwill to all'. As it is today, the world in 1979 was facing much trouble and confusion, but as I listened to the words of the nativity I remember thinking, 'Wow! This is what Christmas is about—the message that we should be striving to share the love, peace, hope and joy that Christ brought to us when he grew up.'

But even when we do recognise that this season is a time of love and peace, that does not mean it is going to be easy to put into practice in the run up to Christmas. When Christmas shopping becomes stressful, when preparations get on top of you, or when the children or grandchildren start arguing over their presents, love and peace might be the last things on your mind! But the peace and love that Christ brought to us were not meant to last for only 24 hours a year. However wonderful the 24-hour truce was during the First World War, the spirit of Christmas should actually last all year round. It should be as important today as it is in the middle of August, or as it will be in just under three weeks' time when Christmas dinner is served!

As it was in 1914, the world is still torn apart by wars; families still feud and fall out over seemingly trivial things; and jealousy, bitterness and hatred are found even among friends and neighbours. But if we really believe that Christmas means something, if we really believe that there is more to the Christmas season than food, drink and presents, then we should embrace Christ's message of love, forgiveness, peace, goodwill and hope. We must promise ourselves that we will put that message into action, not only on Christmas Day, but on every day of the year.

## Reflection

*Think about how busy the run up to Christmas is going to be. Think of the presents you need to buy and wrap, the cards you need to send, the food shopping in hectic supermarkets, the cooking on Christmas Day, the hosting of family and friends, and so on. Now give all your busyness and anxiety to Christ. Say a prayer, asking him to be alongside you over the whole festive season, helping you to stay calm and peaceful. Most of all, ask that he helps you to show love, forgiveness and peace to everyone with whom you come into contact.*

# Finding Christ

## Luke 24:13–19

Two of them were going to a village called Emmaus, about seven miles from Jerusalem. They were talking with each other about everything that had happened. As they talked and discussed these things with each other, Jesus himself came up and walked along with them; but they were kept from recognising him.

He asked them, 'What are you discussing together as you walk along?'

They stood still, their faces downcast. One of them, named Cleopas, asked him, 'Are you the only one visiting Jerusalem who does not know the things that have happened there in these days?'

'What things?' he asked.

'About Jesus of Nazareth,' they replied. 'He was a prophet, powerful in word and deed before God and all the people.'

Every year I eagerly look forward to the summer. You might think that I am a worshipper of the sun and hot weather. In fact, I am actually awaiting the release of the annual superhero blockbuster movies! Whether it's Batman, Superman or Spiderman, I can't get enough of superhero films. One of the things I love most about them is that no one knows who the enigmatic characters behind the masks and costumes actually are. This adds to the suspense and excitement as ordinary human beings such as Bruce Wayne, Clark Kent and

Peter Parker don their special uniforms and save the world in disguise!

In our passage today, two disciples were joined by Jesus as they walked to a place called Emmaus, and they happily chatted away to him. Yet despite the fact that, unlike the superheroes in the summer blockbusters, Jesus wore no special costume or secretive disguise, the disciples still failed to recognise him. They even told him of their deep sadness that their friend had just been crucified, ignorant of the fact that he was walking right beside them! It may all sound rather strange, but how many of us today are like the two disciples, so wrapped up in our own little lives that we fail to recognise Jesus in the midst of them. Even at Christmas time, when we know the real meaning of the season, rarely do we stop and open our hearts and senses to recognise him in our everyday lives.

There is an old Indian story about a young boy who told his father that he had concluded there was no God, as he could not physically see him. The father told his son to find a bowl of water and some salt. Upon his son's return, he asked him to pour the salt into the water, stir it and leave it overnight. The next day, the father asked the son to bring him the salt that he'd put in the water. Of course, the son looked at the bowl and said, 'I can't find the salt, Father; it's dissolved.' So the father ordered him to sip from the bowl and then asked him how it tasted. 'Salty,' the boy answered. The father then told him to throw the water away. The next day he took his son back to where the water had been thrown. The water had, by then, evaporated and the salt had reappeared. 'Like salt in water,' concluded the father, 'we may not be able see God directly in our world, but he is here.'

Christ is not simply someone we will meet at the end of our lives, but that does not mean he continually reveals himself to us in an obvious way. Like salt in water, he is hidden until we taste him. As Elizabeth Barrett Browning puts it:

*Earth's crammed with heaven,*
*And every common bush afire with God:*
*But only he who sees, takes off his shoes,*
*The rest sit round it, and pluck blackberries.*
FROM 'AURORA LEIGH' BY ELIZABETH BARRETT BROWNING (1806–61)

Jesus is in the moments of love, beauty and joy that touch us each day, and so, whenever we experience these things, we experience him. Once we start to recognise Christ in everyday things, we will start to see that he is walking alongside us on our journeys, just as he walked alongside the two disciples on the road to Emmaus. We just need to open our senses to him, looking for him, listening to him, tasting him and touching him.

## Reflection

*Have a think—where do you find love, hope and joy in your life? It might be through friends or family, or music, or watching films, or the beauty of nature, or a beloved pet, or laughter, or even watching or playing sport. Thank God for those times when, each day, he touches your life. This week, you might want to start looking for him in those places where you may not have experienced him before. Try to do something unfamiliar, such as meeting a new person for coffee, learning a new skill, listening to a different genre of music, or simply sitting somewhere new in church and chatting to those around you.*

# 8–14 December

# Christ in our neighbour

My wife hails from Northern Bavaria in Germany and she often waxes lyrical about the things she misses from her home country. As well as the wonderful Christmas celebrations, including the St Nicholas Day revelries, she enthuses about the joyous festivities of St Martin's Day a month or so earlier. Despite the fact that most Protestant churches do not recognise saints' days, the St Martin's Day celebrations have become important even in the Protestant areas of Germany. St Martin of Tours was a Roman soldier who, on one freezing-cold night in the fourth century, was riding his horse in the town of Amiens, in modern-day France. He passed a beggar wearing worn-out, ragged clothes who was so cold that his lips were frozen together and was therefore unable to beg for help. Realising that the beggar was dying, Martin felt compassion towards him, took out his sword and split his warm cloak into two, giving half of it to the poor man. Although not a Christian at that point, Martin was visited by Jesus in a dream that night, and, to his amazement, Jesus was wearing the half-cloak that he had given the beggar. Jesus then turned to all the angels and announced,

'Here is Martin, the Roman soldier who is not baptised; he has clothed me.'

Our call as Christians is both to recognise Jesus in everyone we meet and also to take Jesus to those people. The prologue in John's Gospel talks about the light coming into the world. By following Jesus, we are personally able to bring that light into people's lives. 'I want to be a light that shines for everyone!' St Martin is purported to have once said. Thus the St Martin's Day celebrations in Germany involve lighting bonfires, while children make all sorts of pretty lanterns and process through the town singing songs about the light of God's presence in the world. By recognising Jesus in our neighbours, our light will shine in the darkness and we will be able to treat every person with the compassion, love and respect they deserve. 'I believe in person to person,' wrote Mother Teresa. 'Every person is Christ for me, and since there is only one Jesus, that person is the one person in the world at that moment.'

# Seeing Christ in others

## Matthew 25:34–40

'The King will say to those on his right, "Come, you who are blessed by my Father; take your inheritance, the kingdom prepared for you since the creation of the world. For I was hungry and you gave me something to eat, I was thirsty and you gave me something to drink, I was a stranger and you invited me in, I needed clothes and you clothed me, I was ill and you looked after me, I was in prison and you came to visit me."

'Then the righteous will answer him, "Lord, when did we see you hungry and feed you, or thirsty and give you something to drink? When did we see you a stranger and invite you in, or needing clothes and clothe you? When did we see you ill or in prison and go to visit you?"

'The King will reply, "Truly I tell you, whatever you did for one of the least of these brothers and sisters of mine, you did for me."

In my home town of Penmaenmawr, we have more sheep than people living in the area. When I was younger, an elderly vicar spoke at my local church and told a tale that has stayed with me ever since. A North Wales shepherd is happily grazing his large flock of sheep, when an English tourist stops to admire them. 'That's a wonderful flock you have,' he says. 'How much would you say your sheep walk each day?'

The shepherd answers, 'Which ones, the white ones or the black ones?'

'The white ones,' replies the Englishman.

'Well, the white ones walk around five miles each day,' says the shepherd.

'And the black ones?' asks the tourist.

'Yes, the black ones too,' comes the answer.

'And how much grass would you say they eat daily?' says the Englishman.

'Which ones,' says the shepherd, 'the white or the black?'

'The white ones,' answers the tourist.

'Well, the white ones eat about six pounds of grass each day,' asserts the Welshman.

'And the black ones?' asks the tourist.

'Yes, the black ones too,' comes the answer.

And so the tourist enquires further: 'How much wool would you say they give each year?'

'Which ones, the white or the black?' retorts the shepherd.

'The white ones,' comes the response.

'Well,' he explains, 'I'd say the white ones give some six pounds of wool annually.'

'And the black ones?' asks the Englishman.

'Yes, the black ones too,' comes the answer.

By now the passer-by is curious, so he says, 'I'm sorry, but can I ask why you divide your sheep into white ones and black ones every time you answer one of my questions?'

'Well,' said the shepherd, 'you see that's only natural, because the white ones are actually *my* sheep.'

'Ah,' says the Englishman, 'and what about the black ones?'

And the shepherd answers, 'Yes, the black ones too!'

I have to admit that I can't recall exactly why the elderly

vicar told this tale! But I think it can teach us something about how easily we fall into the trap of relying on the labels that we foist on people around us. The way we see people defines how we act and how we treat each other. As the philosopher Henry David Thoreau wrote, 'The question is not what you look at, but what you see.' In other words, we are constantly wearing spectacles through which we make judgments on people and which distort our attitudes towards them. Yet today's reading urges us to wear Christ-tinted spectacles when we consider each other. In other words, when we look at others, we should be seeing Jesus himself standing in front of us, and because of that we will be able to truly love them as much as they deserve. Thomas Merton recorded in his journal the flash of inspiration he experienced as he walked down a street in Louisville, Kentucky in 1958: 'I was suddenly overwhelmed with the realisation that I loved all these people, that they were mine and I theirs, that we could not be alien to one another even though we were total strangers. It was like waking from a dream of separateness.'

There is no doubt that there are differences between us, many of which are to be celebrated. Our glorious diversity in gender, ethnicity and nationality is certainly a good thing. As Desmond Tutu put it in a speech to the United Nations in 2001: 'How could you have a soccer team if all were goalkeepers? How would it be an orchestra if all were French horns?' This realisation, however, need not lead us to overemphasise our dissimilarities and thus to constantly divide the black sheep from the white sheep. We are all in the same family and in the same flock, and, by wearing Christ-tinted spectacles, we will find our lives change completely. After all, the way we see defines how we act, the things we do, and the way we are with each other. It's only when we see Jesus in others that our actions towards them will become as loving and compassionate as they would be towards Christ himself.

## Reflection

*Consciously think of everyone you meet in the next 24 hours as being Jesus himself – your family, friends, colleagues, shop assistants, even strangers that you pass in the street. Pray that you are able to show as much love, care and compassion towards them as you would towards Christ himself.*

# 9 December

# Love everybody

### Matthew 5:43–48

'You have heard that it was said, "Love your neighbour and hate your enemy." But I tell you, love your enemies and pray for those who persecute you, that you may be children of your Father in heaven. He causes his sun to rise on the evil and the good, and sends rain on the righteous and the unrighteous. If you love those who love you, what reward will you get? Are not even the tax collectors doing that? And if you greet only your own people, what are you doing more than others? Do not even pagans do that? Be perfect, therefore, as your heavenly Father is perfect.'

A few years ago, in the middle of a cold British winter, I took a group of students to the state of Tamil Nadu in southern India, to study the various religions that are to be found in that wonderful country. As I left the airport in Chennai, I was not prepared for the assault on my senses: the dry heat bathed my skin, the beautiful colours dazzled my eyes, and the sounds of the hustle and bustle of the marketplace were a joy to my ears. Neither could anything have prepared me for the poverty and suffering I was immediately to encounter. As I walked towards the market, a young Indian girl came running up to me and put out her hands to beg for money. Her face was disfigured, her skin was dirty and her clothes were torn. There was so much sadness and pain in her eyes, and we were distressed and upset by her and the other beggars, who were asking us for the smallest amounts of money. We were, however, soon taught that we should brush the beggars away with a sharp 'No!' Sadly, if those of us on the visit were completely truthful, we would have to admit that, by the end, the biting mosquitoes bothered us more than the beggars on the street. It became so easy to dehumanise those begging for our help and just ignore them.

Our group's increasingly dismissive attitude towards other people on that trip got me thinking about the acronym that used to adorn many teenage bracelets in America—'WWJD?' ('What would Jesus do?'). This has almost become a parody of itself, with so many Christians and non-Christians now making fun of the WWJD label. It is, however, an important and pertinent question for us to ask in all areas of our lives. In the context of my India trip, I was left asking how Jesus would treat these suffering people we find so easy to ignore. The question is relevant in our own societies and communities, wherever we are living. How would Jesus react to our asylum seekers, the homeless, the poor, the abused, the depressed, the addicted, the persecuted and the disadvantaged?

While I was in India, I became good friends with a young Indian student called Devi. One evening, she invited me to her house for dinner. When I arrived, all her family were there to meet me—mum, dad, brothers, sisters, grandparents, uncles, aunties, cousins—and as I walked in, they took hundreds of photos of this traveller from afar. I felt like a rock star facing the paparazzi! I then sat and chatted for many hours with them, in particular with Devi's grandfather. He told me about a great man he had met when he was younger—who went by the name of Mahatma Gandhi. There are around one billion people in India—15 per cent of the world's population—and I happened to be talking to one of the few living people who had walked and talked with the great Gandhi. He explained to me how Gandhi would travel to different towns and villages around India, but would refuse to stay in the more affluent houses, despite the fact that he'd be able to bath, eat well and sleep comfortably. Instead, he would demand to stay with the 'untouchables', those on the lowest rung of the Indian caste system, in the dirtiest and most impoverished areas. This would naturally shock the village leaders. Yet Gandhi insisted that the poorest of the poor were not untouchable, but were rather *Harijan*— God's children.

Likewise, our own faith teaches us that we are all God's children. No one is viewed as an untouchable in God's kingdom, as God loves everybody—whatever their colour, creed, sexuality, gender, social status or political affiliation. That is why Jesus himself showed love and compassion for all people, whoever they were and whatever they'd done, and he urged us to do the same. Everyone is welcome in God's kingdom, as Jesus demonstrated by showing acceptance and love towards the untouchables of his society—the sick, the poor, the tax collectors, the sinners, the Samaritans, the prostitutes, the lepers and the Gentiles. In the same way, everyone should be welcome in our hearts. What would Jesus do? He would treat every single person as a child of God, so our call is to follow Jesus by loving them that way.

## Reflection

*I once heard Tony Campolo speak and he ended the talk with a challenging sentence: 'We are all willing to do what Jesus wants us to do, but only up to a point.' Take some time to consider what he meant by this. Being completely truthful with yourself, consider the following questions: How easy is it to love our enemies? How easy is it for us to love those whom society encourages us to look down upon? WWJD? How easy is it for us to do what Jesus did?*

# 10 December

# Prejudice

## Luke 7:37–43

A woman in that town who lived a sinful life learned that Jesus was eating at the Pharisee's house, so she came there with an alabaster jar of perfume. As she stood behind him at his feet weeping, she began to wet his feet with her tears. Then she wiped them with her hair, kissed them and poured perfume on them.

When the Pharisee who had invited him saw this, he said to himself, 'If this man were a prophet, he would know who is touching him and what kind of woman she is – that she is a sinner.'

Jesus answered him, 'Simon, I have something to tell you.'

'Tell me, teacher,' he said.

'Two people owed money to a certain money-lender. One owed him five hundred denarii, and the other fifty. Neither of them had the money to pay him back, so he forgave the debts of both. Now which of them will love him more?'

Simon replied, 'I suppose the one who had the bigger debt forgiven.'

'You have judged correctly,' Jesus said.

The author Anaïs Nin once said that 'we don't see things as they are, we see things as *we* are.' In other words, we bring our own particular backgrounds, upbringings and viewpoints to bear on every person we meet and any issue we deal with. This fact dawned on me when I was still quite young. In

1981, as a feisty nine-year-old Welsh boy, I declared myself on a hunger strike. I would not eat again, I told my mum, until she promised to boycott South African food because of the government-supported apartheid there. I was just as zealous in the small school that I attended: I picketed the front gate, with big banners condemning the poor dinner ladies for giving us South African apples. Then one day we had a non-school-uniform day, and I remember a friend of mine wore the one thing you never wear to a Welsh-speaking school in Snowdonia—the England rugby shirt! I am ashamed to say that I was horrible to that poor friend of mine, from the moment I saw him by the school gates in the morning until the school bell signalled it was time to go home. It was only later on that evening that it suddenly dawned on me that, despite my fervent fight against apartheid abroad, in my own way I was certainly not immune to showing blind prejudice and hostility towards others. As C.S. Lewis put it in *The Magician's Nephew* (1955): 'What you see and hear depends a good deal on where you are standing.'

All of us have our own prejudices, and many of these are hidden, sometimes even from ourselves! If we had been at Simon the Pharisee's house in our reading today, it's easy to think we would have been on Jesus' side, accepting and loving as he did. If we were really truthful to ourselves, though, the reality is that most of us would actually have been like the other partygoers. We'd be saying, 'Well, we all know how she got the money for that perfume.' Even if we were a bit more accepting and forgiving of her, we might still consider ourselves moral, upstanding citizens, and so we'd be thinking that we were just that little bit better than this woman 'who lived a sinful life'.

At times all of us look down upon other people. However

much we know in our hearts that the real 'baddies' in the gospel narratives are the hypocritical Pharisees, most of us, at one time or another, have been modern-day Pharisees. Philip Yancey tells the story of a prostitute who came in tears to a friend of his, with a sordid story of drugs, prostitution and abuse. The friend asked if she had ever considered going to a church for help. 'Church!' she exclaimed. 'Why would I ever go there? I'm already feeling terrible about myself. They'd just make me feel worse.' Many people have backgrounds as traumatic as that prostitute's, yet we tend to judge them directly on what we see them do or how we see them act. But Christ was the very last person to make judgments on how people looked, what they did or how they acted. He mixed with tax collectors, prostitutes, Gentiles, Samaritans, lepers and all sorts of so-called 'sinners'. It is only when we humble ourselves and admit our outward and our hidden biases that Christ can help us to be like him—to recognise the beauty and worth of everyone we meet over the Christmas period and beyond.

## Reflection

*Take some time out today to sit and pray about any prejudice you might hold in your heart. You might want to start your prayer with the following words: 'I admit it, Lord, that I am sometimes a modern-day Pharisee. I admit that I often look down on other people – because of how they look or because of what they do. So help me, Lord; help me to learn to be more like you. Help me to look at every person in a loving and non-judgmental way. Help me to recognise that they have had a different background and a different upbringing from me, and help me not to think I'm better than them, but, rather, help me to recognise your face in every person I meet.'*

# Serving

## Philippians 2:6–11

*Being in very nature God,*
*[Christ Jesus] did not consider equality with God*
*something to be used to his own advantage;*
*rather, he made himself nothing*
*by taking the very nature of a servant,*
*being made in human likeness.*

*And being found in appearance as a man,*
*he humbled himself*
*by becoming obedient to death –*
*even death on a cross!*

*Therefore God exalted him to the highest place*
*and gave him the name that is above every name,*
*that at the name of Jesus every knee should bow,*
*in heaven and on earth and under the earth,*
*and every tongue acknowledge that Jesus Christ is Lord,*
*to the glory of God the Father.*

When I was growing up, we only had one small TV in our house, so you can probably imagine the arguments that used to kick off about what the Hughes family would watch each evening. Those dads among you will probably relate to the fact that my dad seemed to have the remote control surgically attached to his hand. So, of course, we watched what Dad chose. Every Sunday evening we were forced to endure the same programme—*Jeeves and Wooster*. This was a typically British comedy, starring Hugh Laurie and Stephen Fry, adapted from P.G. Wodehouse's 'Jeeves' stories. Bertie Wooster was a wealthy English gentleman, who was proud to be a member of the 'idle rich'. Jeeves, on the other hand, was his trusted servant, or, as he described himself, the 'gentleman's personal gentleman'. Jeeves turned out to be the ultimate problem-solver, always extricating his bumbling buffoon of a master from potential disasters. I think I would probably enjoy the series now, but at the time I was a rebellious teenager who would have much preferred to be watching MTV or a sports channel!

From my experience of *Jeeves and Wooster*, I always thought I had inside knowledge of what the Bible meant when it urged us to follow Jesus into servanthood. Despite being a servant, Jeeves seemed to be having rather a pleasant life. Whatever he faced, he seemed to be in control of the situation and, by staying cool and calm, he would always come out on top. The life of a sevant didn't seem particularly difficult or sacrificial to me. In reality, of course, the TV series gave me a false and idealised view of being a servant. Servanthood is not all fun and frivolity. As the suffering servant passages of Isaiah show us, servanthood includes suffering alongside success, despair alongside delight (see, for example, Isaiah 49:4–6). It will often mean humbling ourselves and taking up our cross. 'For it is the one who is least among you all who is the greatest,' asserted Jesus in Luke 9:48.

As we meet people in our daily lives, it is important that we recognise how we, as Christians, should relate to them. We are their servants. This does not mean that we should let them walk all over us. Rather, we are their servants because we recognise the face of our Master in each and every one of them, and thus we show them the kind of love and compassion we would show Christ himself. The inspiring Anglican priest and author Alan Ecclestone went as far as challenging Anglican priests about where they bow at the end of each service. Surely, he says, they should be bowing where they truly believe Christ is? Should they bow to the altar, then? Or to the bread? Perhaps, he suggests, they should be bowing to the congregation. After all, they are the body of Christ.

Servanthood is at the crux of the gospel message. This was what Jesus taught the disciples when he washed their feet at the Last Supper, and it is what he taught us all when 'he humbled himself… even [to] death on a cross'. This is what has scattered the proud, lifted the humble, filled the hungry and brought down the mighty from their thrones. The most wonderful thing is that all of us, whoever we are and wherever we are, can reveal God's glory through our service to our neighbours. As Martin Luther King put it, in a sermon delivered only two months before his death:

*Everybody can be great, because everybody can serve. You don't have to have a college degree to serve. You don't have to make your subject and your verb agree to serve. You don't have to know about Plato and Aristotle to serve. You don't have to know Einstein's theory of relativity to serve. You don't have to know the second theory of thermodynamics in physics to serve. All you need is a heart full of grace and a soul generated by love.*

## Reflection
*Over the next few days, make servanthood your priority. In whatever situation you are, and whoever you are with, consider how you can serve in a compassionate and caring way. Contemplate*

*Augustine's words: 'Your best servant is the person who does not attend so much to hearing what he himself wants, as to willing what he has heard from you.'*

# 12 December

# Helping

**Colossians 3:12–17**

As God's chosen people, holy and dearly loved, clothe yourselves with compassion, kindness, humility, gentleness and patience. Bear with each other and forgive one another if any of you has a grievance against someone. Forgive as the Lord forgave you. And over all these virtues put on love, which binds them all together in perfect unity.

Let the peace of Christ rule in your hearts, since as members of one body you were called to peace. And be thankful. Let the message of Christ dwell among you richly as you teach and admonish one another with all wisdom through psalms, hymns, and songs from the Spirit, singing to God with gratitude in your hearts. And whatever you do, whether in word or deed, do it all in the name of the Lord Jesus, giving thanks to God the Father through him.

A few years back, I visited Australia to give a lecture at the University of Sydney. My memory of my first week 'Down Under' is hazy, to say the least. I suffered from the most appalling jetlag, which meant I was awake all night, wandering around the university campus with the friendly possums, and then trying desperately not to fall asleep during the day! I do remember one incident very clearly, though. I was walking down the high street of the wonderfully named town of Wagga Wagga when, out of the blue, a young teenager came up to me and, without saying a word, put a piece of paper into my hand. Before I knew it, she had disappeared, and I looked down to read the following words:

*Christ has no body but yours,*
*No hands, no feet on earth but yours,*
*Yours are the eyes with which he looks*
*Compassion on this world,*
*Yours are the feet with which he walks to do good,*
*Yours are the hands, with which he blesses all the world.*
*Yours are the hands, yours are the feet,*
*Yours are the eyes, you are his body.*
*Christ has no body now but yours,*
*No hands, no feet on earth but yours,*
*Yours are the eyes with which he looks*
*compassion on this world.*
*Christ has no body now on earth but yours.*
ST TERESA OF AVILA (1515–82)

Those words had a huge effect on me then, and they still inspire me now. I have since discovered that they were written by the 16th-century Spanish contemplative Teresa of Avila, who urged those around her to become Christ to their suffering neighbours by actively showing them love, kindness and compassion.

Sometimes we fear helping others as we believe we will be giving too much of our time and effort without getting anything in return. It is of little surprise that a government report only ten years ago suggested that very few British adults are involved in voluntary work, with young adults being the least likely to engage in such selfless acts. I remember news reports of the time bewailing modern society's loss of community, and its decreasing number of altruistic ventures.

Yet my own experience tells me the outlook might not be quite as bleak as we feared. In the university where I am chaplain, increasing numbers of students are signing up for voluntary work at the Student Volunteer Centre. The work they become involved in is worthwhile and varied—some choose to spend time with disadvantaged young people, some assist at after-school clubs, some help at hospitals and hospices, and some get involved in environmental projects. They do all this alongside their busy timetables of academic studies and any paid work they do to fund their learning.

When I speak to the students about the voluntary work they undertake, they all seem to say the same thing—that, in helping others, they feel they are gaining far more than they are giving. In fact, scientific research supports their belief, revealing that doing good deeds can bring us direct satisfaction and helping others can lift our spirits and bring purpose to our own lives. Still, the New Testament is far more concerned with how our actions benefit others, rather than with their consequences on our own lives. Care, love and compassion are integral to the Christian life, and so when we serve people, we serve God. Although the 16th-century reformers rightly reminded us that we are not saved by good deeds, our acts of kindness are still important, as the call to become Christ to those around us is very much part and parcel of our faith: 'Clothe yourselves with compassion, kindness, humility, gentleness and patience.'

## Reflection
*Make it your priority to carry out a good deed in the next 24 hours. You might decide to visit an elderly or lonely neighbour, to do the shopping for someone who needs help, to treat a friend to lunch, or to spend some time picking up litter from*

*your local park. It need not be something big, but simply an 'act of random kindness', as the character Evan Baxter put it in the film* Evan Almighty *(2007).*

# Courage

## Luke 10:25–37

On one occasion an expert in the law stood up to test Jesus. 'Teacher,' he asked, 'what must I do to inherit eternal life?'

'What is written in the Law?' he replied. 'How do you read it?'

He answered, '"Love the Lord your God with all your heart and with all your soul and with all your strength and with all your mind"; and, "Love your neighbour as yourself."'

'You have answered correctly,' Jesus replied. 'Do this and you will live.'

But he wanted to justify himself, so he asked Jesus, 'And who is my neighbour?'

In reply Jesus said: 'A man was going down from Jerusalem to Jericho, when he was attacked by robbers. They stripped him of his clothes, beat him and went away, leaving him half-dead. A priest happened to be going down the same road, and when he saw the man, he passed by on the other side. So too, a Levite, when he came to the place and saw him, passed by on the other side. But a Samaritan, as he travelled, came where the man was; and when he saw him, he took pity on him. He went to him and bandaged his wounds, pouring on oil and wine. Then he put the man on his own donkey, brought him to an inn and took care of him. The next day he took out two denarii and gave them to the innkeeper. "Look after him," he said, "and when I return, I will reimburse you for any extra expense you may have."

'Which of these three do you think was a neighbour to the man who fell into the hands of robbers?'

The expert in the law replied, 'The one who had mercy on him.'

Jesus told him, 'Go and do likewise.'

As Christians we need courage each day of our lives. Sometimes it is the courage to stand up for our convictions; at other times it is the courage to tell someone of our faith. On many occasions, we are called to have the courage simply to stand alongside others, just as the Good Samaritan supported the robbed and beaten man. The real challenge of our faith is to 'love our neighbour', and so be brave enough to support those in need and to stand up for those who face suffering or injustice, either in our society or in others across the world. We are not guaranteed an easy ride. We may find ourselves facing ridicule, pain, prejudice or hostility. Even the Good Samaritan, by stopping to help, was risking being attacked himself.

Down the years, many individuals have stood up against injustice and oppression, and have even found themselves struggling and on the brink of failure. Some have paid the ultimate price of their lives through their brave stances. Ninoy Aquino, for example, stood up for freedom by opposing the bloody dictatorship of President Marcos in the Philippines in the 1970s. After being imprisoned for many years in his home country, he escaped to the US, where he informed the world of the corruption and extravagance of the Marcos regime. In 1983, Aquino decided to return to the Philippines, fully aware that he almost certainly faced either imprisonment or death. In an interview only 24 hours before his flight, he told foreign journalists: 'If my fate is to die by an assassin's bullet, so be it. But I cannot be petrified by inaction or fear of assassination and therefore stay in a corner.' His words were to prove prophetic. As he descended the steps of the plane in Manila, shots rang out and, minutes later, he lay dead on the airport's tarmac. Yet this tragic event was not the end of the story, as his sacrificial act heralded huge change in his beloved country. Within three short years, the 'People Power Revolution', as it became known, had toppled the Marcos regime and a new president, Aquino's wife Cory Aquino, brought a new era of freedom and peace to the Philippines.

We ourselves may rarely, if ever, be faced with such extreme situations. Still, the drive and perseverance of such modern-day heroes can encourage us in our smaller struggles. Likewise, the stories in our scriptures can inspire us—from Moses leading the slaves out of Egypt, through the exile by the rivers of Babylon, to the apostle Paul and his friends facing persecution, incarceration and shipwreck. Jesus is the ultimate example of this. He opposed injustice by championing God's compassion and peace, even though it meant he became a suffering servant and was persecuted and killed. Yet that was not the end of the story. Three days later, his resurrection was a triumph over the powers of evil and oppression. When we support those who are suffering, and find ourselves treading a lonely path and taking up our cross, we can always be reassured that resurrections do, indeed, follow crucifixions.

## Reflection

*Reflect on any support you have given to national or international campaigns to help those who are struggling for freedom from poverty or oppression. Consider any times when you have opposed local instances of racism, homophobia, bullying or prejudice that you have seen people encountering. Pray that*

*God gives you the strength and courage to stand up for those who are suffering and to make a real difference with acts of kindness and compassion.*

# Shared humanity

### Genesis 11:1–9

Now the whole world had one language and a common speech. As people moved eastward, they found a plain in Shinar and settled there.

They said to each other, 'Come, let's make bricks and bake them thoroughly.' They used brick instead of stone, and bitumen for mortar. Then they said, 'Come, let us build ourselves a city, with a tower that reaches to the heavens, so that we may make a name for ourselves; otherwise we will be scattered over the face of the whole earth.'

But the Lord came down to see the city and the tower the people were building. The Lord said, 'If as one people speaking the same language they have begun to do this, then nothing they plan to do will be impossible for them. Come, let us go down and confuse their language so they will not understand each other.'

So the Lord scattered them from there over all the earth, and they stopped building the city. That is why it was called Babel—because there the Lord confused the language of the whole world. From there the Lord scattered them over the face of the whole earth.

Recently, on my way to visit my wife's family in Northern Bavaria, I spent a few days in Berlin. It's a lively and attractive capital, with so much to offer visitors and sightseers. Yet not so long ago it was a very different place. On the morning of

13 August 1961, the city woke up divided. Troops in East Germany had erected six-foot-high wire fences and traffic between East and West Germany was stopped. The wire fence was soon replaced by a concrete wall, and over the next three decades hundreds of Germans were killed or injured trying to cross it. Many of us will remember the scenes of jubilation on 9 November 1989 when the gates of the wall were finally opened and large sections of the wall itself were torn down by ecstatic crowds.

We humans certainly have a tendency to divide ourselves up and concentrate on what separates us. We may even find ourselves building walls in our hearts and our minds. It's so tempting to divide our worlds into 'us' and 'them' and to view those who are different from us as insignificant, inferior or flawed. This occurs most worryingly with the blight of xenophobic or racist hatred, but religions also can descend into such rigid and arrogant thinking. Such divisions can even take place at a more trivial level, when we affirm our fervent loyalty for our beloved football team, a particular type of music or a brand of clothing.

In our desire to affirm our own beliefs and worldviews, we must always hold on to our shared humanity. After all, we have far more in common with each other than we have things that separate us. One of my favourite films is *Dances with Wolves* (1990), which won seven Oscars and was nominated for many more. It tells the story of Lieutenant John Dunbar, played by Kevin Costner, who was sent to a remote outpost in the Dakotan wilderness during the American Civil War. There, he encounters the local Sioux tribe and gradually learns their language, befriends them and is accepted into their community. 'Nothing I have been told about these people is correct,' Dunbar muses at one point. 'They are not thieves or beggars; they are not the bogeymen they are made out to be.' Rather than reaffirming the prejudices of the new American settlers, Dunbar discovers his similarity to and common humanity with the indigenous tribe.

Our reading today is the story of the Tower of Babel. This tale suggests that the root of our disunity is to be found in our pride, in our desire for fame and fortune, and in our mistaken belief that we do not need God in our lives. In reality it is only with God and through God that we can truly find fulfilment ourselves and connect with others around us. Earlier in the book of Genesis, humanity had been created 'in the image of God', reminding us that we have one source and that source is the very foundation of our unity. As Thomas Aquinas put it, 'God is in all things, yes he reigns in the very heart of all things.' While still celebrating, treasuring and sharing our differences, we must never forget our common humanity and our essential unity in our Father.

## Reflection

*Are you building any 'towers' in your life? Most of us hanker after one thing or another, whether that is fame, recognition, wealth, excitement or success. In prayer, give over your worldly desires to God and ask that whatever you do or achieve in life, he helps you do this for his glory, not your own.*

*As you go about your day and meet different people, whether they are people you know well or strangers, try actively to recognise your shared humanity with them, rather than dwell on your differences.*

# 15–21 December

# Christic in the natural world

*Joy to the world! the Lord is come;*
*Let earth receive her King;*
*Let every heart prepare him room,*
*And heaven and nature sing,*
*And heaven and nature sing,*
*And heaven, and heaven, and nature sing.*

*Joy to the world! the Saviour reigns;*
*Let men their songs employ;*
*While fields and floods, rocks, hills and plains*
*Repeat the sounding joy,*
*Repeat the sounding joy,*
*Repeat, repeat the sounding joy.*

FROM 'JOY TO THE WORLD' BY ISAAC WATTS (1674–1748)
(BASED ON PSALM 98)

By this week many of us will have had a few
Christmas cards fall through our letter boxes. If you
have them close by, take a look at the pictures that
adorn them. There is a good chance that a number
of them will depict scenes from nature. There may
be a beautiful snow-filled landscape or a small robin

searching for food in the snow. Every year I receive a
Christmas card from a friend in Australia, on which,
interestingly, pictures of landscapes and animals
still figure prominently, although they are depicted
very differently from those in the UK. On Australian
Christmas cards, the snowy hills are replaced by
beautiful beaches and rolling seas, while the robins
and reindeers are replaced by koalas and kangaroos.
It always amuses me that, very often, the animals are
wearing Santa Claus hats and the beach scenes often
depict Father Christmas in Bermuda shorts, happily
surfing on six-foot waves!

Whether in the northern or southern hemisphere,
Christmas is often related to the natural world.
Both heaven *and* nature sing when Jesus is born,
according to the much-loved carol 'Joy to the world'.
In scripture, the birth of Christ is very much rooted in
its environment. There is the journey to Bethlehem,
the shepherds in the fields and the star in the sky.
In nativity retellings, we often embellish the scene
even further. For a number of years, Christians in
Cardiff have organised a 'live nativity' in the city
centre, with a real-life donkey drawing much of the
attention. Christians in Hull have recently taken this
one step further, with numerous other animals joining
the donkey in their nativity, including three real-life
camels!

We shouldn't be surprised at how integral nature
is to our celebration of Christmas. The incarnation,
after all, was not just about the relationship between
God and humanity. The early Old Testament
covenants were between God and all of his creation

(Genesis 9:17), and the new covenant in Christ offers salvation to the whole cosmos (Colossians 1:20). Christmas is, therefore, a great opportunity for us to open our eyes to things we often take for granted and to marvel at the wonder of the natural world around us. As the 16th-century reformer Martin Luther stated, 'God writes the gospel not in the Bible alone, but on trees and flowers and clouds and stars.'

# Incarnation and the wider world

### Colossians 1:15–20

The Son is the image of the invisible God, the firstborn over all creation. For in him all things were created: things in heaven and on earth, visible and invisible, whether thrones or powers or rulers or authorities; all things have been created through him and for him. He is before all things, and in him all things hold together. And he is the head of the body, the church; he is the beginning and the firstborn from among the dead, so that in everything he might have the supremacy. For God was pleased to have all his fullness dwell in him, and through him to reconcile to himself all things, whether things on earth or things in heaven, by making peace through his blood, shed on the cross.

Recently I visited Barcelona for the first time. Little could have prepared me for the wonderful sights and sounds of the city. Not least were the two majestic places of worship—the lavish and creative *Sagrada Família*, Antonio Gaudí's *magnum opus* which is still unfinished after 130 years, and the huge city cathedral, with its striking gothic towers reaching up to the sky, as if attempting to hold the hand of God himself. Upon my return to the UK, I visited my youngest brother in the small town of Leighton Buzzard in Bedfordshire. One morning, he announced that he was going to take me to his local cathedral. I feigned enthusiasm, believing that nothing could compare to the Spanish delights I had recently encountered. I was, however, to be astounded by where I was taken. He led me to the Whipsnade 'tree cathedral'. This is not an official, consecrated place of worship, but I found myself connecting with the divine there as much as I had at the opulent buildings in Barcelona.

Whipsnade's incredible cathedral is a collection of trees, hedges and shrubs, planted in the shape and form of a medieval cathedral. As I wandered through the different sections of the cathedral—the lady chapel, the nave, the choir stalls— my senses bathed in God's wonderful creation and I felt my heart lift heavenwards. There was something truly inspiring and uplifting about the fragrance of the foliage, the sweet song of the birds and the visual delight of the autumnal colours. Like my Welsh ancestors in the Celtic tradition, I realised that the entirety of nature is a precious and valuable house of worship, which needs to be nurtured, maintained and appreciated. After all, this magnificent creation is intimately linked with, and brings us closer to, its loving creator.

It is easy for us to forget that the incarnation, which is at the heart of the Christmas story, has far-reaching implications for the whole of creation. As Genesis 1:31 tells us, God regards our world as 'very good'. By entering the world in the person of Christ, God guarantees it his continuing care and ultimate redemption. The resurrection, after all, does not only promise redemption for individuals alone, but for the whole cosmos. As our passage today puts it, 'For God was pleased to have all his fullness dwell in him, and through him to reconcile to himself *all* things, whether things on earth or things in heaven, by making peace through his blood, shed on the cross.'

Thus, the incarnation should define how we view the natural world and how we treat God's precious creation. In his poem 'God's grandeur' (1877), Gerard Manley Hopkins wrote that 'there lives the dearest freshness deep down things'. That 'dearest freshness' is Christ himself: 'All things have been created through him and for him. He is before all things, and in him all things hold together.' The incarnation should inspire us to a global compassion, as we show our love, care and gratitude for, in the words of Francis of Assisi, 'Brother Sun', 'Sister Moon and the stars', 'Brothers Wind and Air', 'Sister Water', and all the rest of our wonderful cosmic family.

## Reflection

*Collect a leaf from your garden or from a local park. Take some time to study it. Notice its colour, its size, the different textures on it and its imperfections. In silence, feel it in your hands. Is it smooth or rough? Warm or cold? Feel its weight and pass it from one hand to the other. Touch it against your face or the back of your hand. Smell its aroma. Explore that leaf. When we view an object like a leaf, it is as if we bring it into being all over again—as if it is being recreated. So, for another moment of silence, remember that this leaf represents the wonder of God's creation. Know that it is dancing and crying out in the presence of God. Experience creation's inherent goodness and open yourselves to the source of this beauty and the sustainer of this delight. Experience the incarnate Christ through this simple little leaf.*

# Nature

**Psalm 148:1–13**

*Praise the Lord.*
*Praise the Lord from the heavens;*
 *praise him in the heights above.*
*Praise him, all his angels;*
 *praise him, all his heavenly hosts.*
*Praise him, sun and moon;*
 *praise him, all you shining stars.*
*Praise him, you highest heavens*
 *and you waters above the skies.*

*Let them praise the name of the Lord,*
 *for at his command they were created,*
*and he established them for ever and ever –*
 *he issued a decree that will never pass away.*

*Praise the Lord from the earth,*
 *you great sea creatures and all ocean depths,*
*lightning and hail, snow and clouds,*
 *stormy winds that do his bidding,*
*you mountains and all hills,*
 *fruit trees and all cedars,*
*wild animals and all cattle,*
 *small creatures and flying birds,*
*kings of the earth and all nations,*
 *you princes and all rulers on earth,*

*young men and women,*
  *old men and children.*

*Let them praise the name of the Lord,*
  *for his name alone is exalted;*
  *his splendour is above the earth and the heavens.*

From the front door of my North Wales childhood home, we'd enjoy wonderful views of the sea, and on a clear day we could see the faint outline of the Isle of Man in the distance. From the back door, we looked out up to the spectacular peaks of the Snowdonia mountains. My older brother was enthralled by the nature surrounding us, and took every opportunity to be outside studying the birds, moths and butterflies. My interests took me in a very different direction. At the age of eleven, I bought an old record player and a collection of LPs in a church jumble sale. Thus began my lifelong addiction to music. But while my friends were bopping to Bananarama or breakdancing to the Beastie Boys, my bedroom was filled with the fiddle and steel guitar of the songs of Johnny Cash and Willie Nelson. Despite Wales being the land of song, my penchant for country music seemed to be quite unique among my compatriots.

When I moved away from my small home town to work in the city of Cardiff, I soon realised how much I had taken my picturesque surroundings for granted. I began to miss those spectacular views and the inspiring countryside, and I would do anything to get back up north, even if only for a weekend. Work was increasingly frantic and stressful, and I would find myself dreaming of purple-headed mountains and long sandy beaches. Then one day, as I was hurrying through my local park on my way to grab a sandwich for lunch, it dawned on me how lovely the simple nature in that small park was. The grass was lush, the trees were swaying in the wind and birds were gliding in the sky. I suddenly felt a sense of calm and peace, and became aware of God's reassuring presence.

Many of us imagine that we have to look forward to a perfect moment to be able to stop and take time to enjoy the world around us. If we could only get away from the hustle and bustle of our everyday lives, or if we could only take a holiday to a scenic destination, then we'd have time to appreciate the wonders of nature. The reality is that wherever we are and whatever we're doing, we can make space to connect with God through our surroundings, even if it's only a quickly grabbed five minutes at lunchtime.

One of my favourite country songs, 'I saw God today' by the Grammy Award winner George Strait, describes how we so often fail to recognise God in the midst of our busy lives. But if we open our eyes to his presence, we will find that his fingerprints are all around us, in every part of his beautiful creation. The song describes God revealing himself to the singer through a fragile flower breaking through the concrete on a city street. Appreciating the natural world has less to do with the amount of beauty that's around us, and more to do with how much we open our eyes to that beauty. We could be walking around the Hanging Gardens of Babylon yet fail to be moved by the stunning foliage, or we could be strolling in our local park and be left awestruck by the trees lining the path. We could even be stuck in our flat and feel uplifted and inspired by a potted plant on our window sill or the sunshine as it illuminates our bed sheets.

These days, if ever I feel stressed or anxious, the first thing I'll do is take a five-minute stroll in the park to calm down. It does not make all my worries go away, but it helps me to put them into perspective as I connect with the creator through his creation. As the Bellamy Brothers, another chart-topping country music group, put it as they describe how they find God through the beauty of nature while fishing on a Sunday morning, 'Jesus ain't no stained-glass window'!

## Reflection
*It need not be a warm and sunny summer's day for you to connect with the divine through nature. Whether it is raining, snowing or sunny, and whether it is warm or cold, take a five-minute walk today and actively notice the beauty of nature all around you, whether in the town or the countryside. Like the Psalmist, praise God for everything you see!*

# Flowers

**Luke 1:46–55**

Mary said:

> 'My soul glorifies the Lord
>   and my spirit rejoices in God my Saviour,
> for he has been mindful
>   of the humble state of his servant.
> From now on all generations will call me blessed,
>   for the Mighty One has done great things for me –
>   holy is his name.
> His mercy extends to those who fear him,
>   from generation to generation.
> He has performed mighty deeds with his arm;
>   he has scattered those who are proud in their inmost
>   thoughts.
> He has brought down rulers from their thrones
>   but has lifted up the humble.
> He has filled the hungry with good things
>   but has sent the rich away empty.
> He has helped his servant Israel,
>   remembering to be merciful
> to Abraham and his descendants for ever,
>   just as he promised our ancestors.'

Some time ago, I took my young daughter to a long service at
our local cathedral in Llandaff, Cardiff. She behaved remark-

ably well, but was very much ready to leave by the end. Then, out of the corner of her eye, she noticed something shining and beautiful in one of the lady chapels there. Behind its small altar is a magnificent reredos screen, with twelve delightful sculptures made from gilt bronze. Each of these sculptures is of a flower whose Welsh name references the Virgin Mary. Such a practice was popular during the Middle Ages. (The English word 'marigold' originated as a result of these flowers being placed around statues of Mary instead of gold coins, at which point they became known as 'Mary's gold', which in turn became 'marigolds'.) Today, it is largely modern Welsh names for flowers that are taught to children in schools. Still, my daughter remained transfixed by the traditional Welsh names and the sculptures of the flowers. There was *clustog Fair* (Mary's ears) for thrift; *esgid Fair* (Mary's shoes) for monkshood; *ysgol Fair* (Mary's ladder) for cornflower; *gwniadur Mair* (Mary's thimble) for foxglove; and *chwys Fair* (Mary's sweat) for buttercup. Although the sculptor, Frank Roper, is known to be unconventional and eccentric, even he saw fit not to include *llaeth bron Mair* (lungwort), which translates as 'Mary's breast milk'!

While walking back home from the cathedral along Cardiff's Taff Trail, my daughter and I attempted to find some of the flowers we had seen on that reredos. As we did so, she asked me a stream of questions about Jesus' mother. Not everyone has a Catholic background, so Mary does not necessarily play a prominent part in our faith. But whatever our personal theological or church experience, Mary can certainly be cherished as a wonderful example of faith in action. To lift the title from a popular film of the 1990s, there's something about Mary! During the Christmas period, we remember that this young Jewish girl must have been so fearful when she discovered she was expecting—fearful of rejection, fearful of humiliation and fearful of the pain of childbirth. Yet she turned difficulty on its head by trusting God, putting herself completely in his hands and embracing the wonder of life. In our passage today, she actively praises him for giving her the honour of bearing his Son. She was, according to the reformer Martin Luther, a paragon of faithfulness, whose importance in the Christmas story, and in the subsequent life story of Jesus, must never be ignored.

At the same time, we must never consider Mary's wonderful, life-affirming way of approaching struggles and difficulties as something to recall only during the Christmas period. Poet Kathleen Norris, in reminiscing about the attitude to Mary in her childhood church, warns of this danger: 'We dragged Mary out at Christmas along with the angels and placed her at centre stage, then we packed her safely in the crèche box for the rest of the year.' Instead of leaving Mary behind after our Christmas celebrations, we should be embracing her life and words throughout the year. Traditionally, our passage today has been used as a canticle (entitled the Magnificat) in evening prayer services in Catholic, Lutheran and Anglican churches worldwide. In it, Mary champions some of those things that are important in Christ's kingdom—not power, but service; not oppression, but mercy; not riches, but love. Although the Magnificat is not used daily in all churches, the sight of flowers as we pass them each day in parks and gardens, or simply in vases on our windowsills, can serve instead to remind us of the love, faithfulness and service to which Mary's words and life attest.

## Reflection

*Flowers are fragile. They face all kinds of adversities and break through soil into all sorts of harsh environments. Still, they grow to bring colour and beauty to the world and they lift our mood, especially when we are suffering. Perhaps this is one of the reasons why people bring us flowers when we are ill or grieving. Consider Mary's faithful role in the Christmas story, despite the difficulties and fear she was facing, and dwell on the importance of her uplifting words in today's passage. Ask God for the strength and confidence to face your own times of worry and anxiety, secure in the knowledge of his care and love for you.*

# 18 December

# Trees

**Luke 2:1–7**

In those days Caesar Augustus issued a decree that a census should be taken of the entire Roman world. (This was the first census that took place while Quirinius was governor of Syria.) And everyone went to their own town to register.

So Joseph also went up from the town of Nazareth in Galilee to Judea, to Bethlehem the town of David, because he belonged to the house and line of David. He went there to register with Mary, who was pledged to be married to him and was expecting a child. While they were there, the time came for the baby to be born, and she gave birth to her firstborn, a son. She wrapped him in cloths and placed him in a manger, because there was no guest room available for them.

When I started teaching 20 years ago, I knew very little about the students who attended my lectures. The miracle of Facebook has changed the situation considerably. No sooner has a student added me to his or her account than my Facebook newsfeed begins informing me of their interests, friends, families, holiday destinations and nights out. Sometimes I discover information about them that I would prefer not to know, but more often Facebook gives me a privileged glimpse into their lives. Recently, I noticed that a student of mine was continually posting pictures of trees on her Facebook page. When I next saw her, I casually enquired about this fact. The enthusiasm of her response was well beyond anything I had expected.

She explained that her obsession with trees affected every part of her life. Her bedroom is decorated in lime green, with a large tree painted in the corner, right over the pillow end of her bed. While she lies in bed, snuggled up in the imagined shade of this huge oak tree, she reads books about trees and writes poetry and prose about their beauty and wonder. Then, during the daytime, she will visit her favourite trees in the local park or go for more extensive walks in woodland. She described the fresh forest smell, the colour that enlivens bleak spaces and the wonderful intricacies of the leaves and branches. She told me that she also undertakes trips to find particularly rare species of trees, or to bask in the spectacle of famous, heritage trees, such as the 1500 year-old yew at Much Marcle in Herefordshire. She even informed me that you can order maps from the Woodland Trust detailing exactly where to find the most interesting trees of the British countryside.

In hearing my student wax lyrical about trees, I gradually realised that her relationship with them was not incidental. Rather, it was deeply spiritual and incarnational. As a child, she had been drawn to trees because they represented pillars of stability, fidelity and dependability in the midst of an increasingly confusing world. They soon came to reflect her increasingly intimate relationship with God. Trees gave her, she claimed, a privileged view into the Father's heart, which is unchanging no matter how we're feeling or how exciting or miserable our life may be. By relating the divine to her love for trees, trees helped her to stay calm through the storms of life and to face things that were weighing heavily on her mind.

Numerous trees are described in the Bible—from the tree of the knowledge of good and evil in the Garden of Eden and the majestic cedars of Lebanon used in building Solomon's Temple, to the trees which rejoice in the presence of God in the book of Isaiah and the healing tree of the book of Revelation. Jesus would have had a particularly intimate relationship with trees because he was brought up learning his father's trade of carpentry (Mark 6:3). It is fitting, then, that at both the beginning and the end of his life, wood plays a prominent role—in his manger and in his cross. As I walked away from chatting about trees to my student, she called after me, 'Trees really can bring us so much love and healing.' As we think of the first Christmas, and what that baby in a wooden manger would grow up to do for us, we should certainly be thanking God for blessing us with trees.

## Reflection

*Go for a short walk in the park or in the countryside (or, if you cannot get out, look out of your window) and notice the beautiful variety of trees that you pass—their shapes and their colours, whether they have lost their leaves or not. Now find a particular tree to adopt as 'your' tree. Spend some time with that tree, feel its bark, smell its aroma, and notice its colours. As you stand close to that tree, pray through some of your worries and concerns, asking God to bring comfort and healing. If you live close to your tree, try to return to it from time to time, to pray and to leave any anxieties that you are feeling at the foot of the manger/cross.*

# Birds

## Mark 1:1–11

The beginning of the good news about Jesus the Messiah, the Son of God, as it is written in Isaiah the prophet:

*'I will send my messenger ahead of you,*
  *who will prepare your way' –*
*'a voice of one calling in the wilderness,*
*"Prepare the way for the Lord,*
  *make straight paths for him."'*

And so John the Baptist appeared in the wilderness, preaching a baptism of repentance for the forgiveness of sins. The whole Judean countryside and all the people of Jerusalem went out to him. Confessing their sins, they were baptised by him in the River Jordan. John wore clothing made of camel's hair, with a leather belt round his waist, and he ate locusts and wild honey. And this was his message: 'After me comes the one more powerful than I, the straps of whose sandals I am not worthy to stoop down and untie. I baptise you with water, but he will baptise you with the Holy Spirit.'

At that time Jesus came from Nazareth in Galilee and was baptised by John in the Jordan. Just as Jesus was coming up out of the water, he saw heaven being torn open and the Spirit descending on him like a dove. And a voice came from heaven: 'You are my Son, whom I love; with you I am well pleased.'

My elder brother is only 18 months older than me, but we grew up with very different interests. While I was riding my BMX bikes, playing computer games, listening to music and writing painfully miserable poetry, he had only one real interest and that was bird-watching. In fact, by the time he was 18 years old he had grown into a self-confessed 'twitcher', travelling many miles simply to see birds that he had not seen before, so he could tick them off his 'life list'. We would often hear the beep of his small pager, which would inform him where the latest rare bird had been spotted, whereupon he would jump into his car and travel across the country for a brief glimpse of some rarity or other.

Each year as the postman drops Christmas cards with pictures of robin redbreasts on them through our letterbox, I remember my brother, who at that early hour of the morning is probably outside 'sea-watching' in the harsh cold. In other words, he will be sitting on a cliff edge, staring into his telescope, scanning the horizon, in the hope that some rare bird, blown in from America, is flying past. Those robins on the Christmas cards also serve to remind me of the special place that birds have always had in the Christian tradition. The Bible is littered with allusions to these feathered creatures, from the birds that Noah sent out from the ark and the raven that brought food to the prophet Elijah, to the references to doves and sparrows in the Gospels. Birds also filled the lives of many of the saints. Both Cuthbert of Lindisfarne and Francis of Assisi became renowned for their love of birds. Cuthbert reputedly enacted the first bird-protection laws in England, as he tried to safeguard his beloved eider ducks from harm.

While most of us are neither twitchers nor saints, birds can still inspire us and bring us comfort and peace of mind. One of my favourite passages of scripture presents the love and care of God in ornithological terms. Here God is described as covering us with his pinions and giving us refuge under his wings (Psalm 91:4). This passage became particularly important to me a few years back, when I was diagnosed with a degenerative spinal condition and had to undergo major back surgery. As I lay in bed, recovering from the operation, I would read this psalm aloud and visualise being brought into the warm safehold of God's presence. It did not take my suffering away, but it certainly allayed some of my fears and worries. Jesus points to the birds in the air to encourage us to put our concerns into perspective (Matthew 6:26). It is of little surprise, then, that the symbol of the Holy Spirit is a bird—the lowly, yet graceful, dove, which also adorns many of our Christmas cards. So, as we pray at Christmas for 'peace on earth', we also ask the Spirit to bring peace to our hearts and to calm our personal anxieties.

## Reflection

*Spend some time watching birds—on a walk, from your window or simply on a wildlife programme on the television or internet. Notice how calm they seem. Despite all the dangers they face, they do not seem to worry or get stressed. As Elizabeth Cheney wrote in her poem 'Overheard in an orchard':*

> *Said the robin to the sparrow,*
> *'I should surely like to know*
> *Why these anxious human beings*
> *Rush about and worry so.'*

*Imagine yourself being taken under God's wing, into his protection and care. Quietly, in your heart, ask the God who holds you so closely to help bring you peace and to calm any fears that you are harbouring.*

# Animals

### Job 39:1–12

*'Do you know when the mountain goats give birth?*
*Do you watch when the doe bears her fawn?*
*Do you count the months till they bear?*
*Do you know the time they give birth?*
*They crouch down and bring forth their young;*
*their labour pains are ended.*
*Their young thrive and grow strong in the wilds;*
*they leave and do not return.*

*'Who let the wild donkey go free?*
*Who untied its ropes?*
*I gave it the wasteland as its home,*
*the salt flats as its habitat.*
*It laughs at the commotion in the town;*
*it does not hear a driver's shout.*
*It ranges the hills for its pasture*
*and searches for any green thing.*

*'Will the wild ox consent to serve you?*
*Will it stay by your manger at night?*
*Can you hold it to the furrow with a harness?*
*Will it till the valleys behind you?*
*Will you rely on it for its great strength?*
*Will you leave your heavy work to it?*
*Can you trust it to haul in your grain*
*and bring it to your threshing floor?'*

Meetings are not my favourite aspect of work. However, if those meetings are one-to-one in a coffee shop, they become far more pleasurable! One of my most memorable meetings over a cup of frothy coffee was when I was blessed to spend an hour with bestselling author and President Clinton's former spiritual adviser Tony Campolo. As he was one of my theological heroes, I was keen to make a good impression. Still, I told myself that I must not simply agree with everything he said, to avoid coming across as a 'yes man'. Before long, our conversation turned to the incarnation and, in particular, its implications on the natural world. He told me about a film entitled *Little Big Man* (1970), which he had watched when he was younger. I immediately announced that I would order it on DVD to watch. He leaned across and whispered, 'It's not a good film, Trystan.' I therefore revised my earlier enthusiasm and reassured him that I would not rush to watch it. 'It's not a good film, Trystan,' he repeated, but then added with a twinkle in his eye, 'because it's a great film!' He laughed out loud as my 'yes man' status was complete and I reverted to my original eagerness to watch the film!

When I returned home I did indeed order the film and thoroughly enjoyed watching it. Little Big Man, played by Dustin Hoffman, is an orphaned white boy who is brought up as a Cheyenne Native American. Upon his return to living among the white settlers, they try to persuade him to use his Cheyenne tracking skills to help make them rich. He is expected to locate buffalo, which would be slaughtered for their hides. 'There's a world of money chewing grass on those plains,' one character tells him. Little Big Man, however, refuses to endanger the increasingly scarce buffalo, because his adoptive family had always taught him the ultimate value of living things. 'The white men,' his Cheyenne grandfather explained, 'they believe everything is dead—stone, earth, animals and people. If things keep trying to live, white men will rub them out.'

It is a sad fact that Christians through history have often lacked care and compassion towards the creatures with which we share the land and the seas. Instead, we have believed that animals were put on earth simply for human exploitation. Yet the pages of scripture display a deeply reverential view of animal life and are brimming with the plethora of weird and wonderful creatures that inhabit planet earth, as shown in today's passage from the book of Job. After everything Job went through, all his pain and suffering, this is how God finally decides to show himself to his servant. He reveals himself as the God of wandering donkeys (vv. 5–8), as well as leaping locusts, snorting horses, flapping ostriches and soaring hawks (see the rest of Job 39).

This hints at how important the natural world is to the divine and how imperative it is for us to have the same view. It is clear from many sections of scripture that God continually watches, loves and cares for his creatures, and he does this not for the sake of us humans, but for their own sake. Scholars inform us that this attitude was quite possibly unique among all the gods of the ancient world, and it has huge implications for our own appreciation and treatment of farm animals, domestic pets and wild animals. We are not placed here to dominate and abuse. Rather, we must take seriously our role as God's partners, as we impart his love to the whole of his creation. 'Until we extend our circle of compassion to include every living creature,' wrote the missionary Albert Schweitzer, 'we cannot enjoy "world peace".'

## Reflection

*Slowly, prayerfully and thoughtfully reflect on the following words by Albert Schweitzer:*

Hear our humble prayer, O God, for our friends the animals, especially for animals who are suffering; for animals that are overworked, underfed and cruelly treated; for all wistful creatures in captivity that beat their wings against bars; for any that are hunted or lost or deserted or frightened or hungry; for all that must be put to death. We entreat for them all Thy mercy and pity, and for those who deal with them we ask a heart of compassion and gentle hands and kindly words. Make us, ourselves, to be true friends to animals, and so to share the blessings of the merciful. Amen.

# The rainbow and the incarnation

### Genesis 9:8–17

Then God said to Noah and to his sons with him: 'I now establish my covenant with you and with your descendants after you and with every living creature that was with you—the birds, the livestock and all the wild animals, all those that came out of the ark with you—every living creature on earth. I establish my covenant with you: never again will all life be destroyed by the waters of a flood; never again will there be a flood to destroy the earth. '

And God said, 'This is the sign of the covenant I am making between me and you and every living creature with you, a covenant for all generations to come: I have set my rainbow in the clouds, and it will be the sign of the covenant between me and the earth. Whenever I bring clouds over the earth and the rainbow appears in the clouds, I will remember my covenant between me and you and all living creatures of every kind. Never again will the waters become a flood to destroy all life. Whenever the rainbow appears in the clouds, I will see it and remember the everlasting covenant between God and all living creatures of every kind on the earth.'

So God said to Noah, 'This is the sign of the covenant I have established between me and all life on the earth.'

One of my favourite things about the festive period is the decorations, and especially the beautiful Christmas trees. Each year, our tree sits proudly in a corner of the living room, as if it's been elevated to full membership of the household—a family tree, if you like! I'll often sit in silence, staring at the twinkling baubles, the sparkling tinsel and, most of all, the dazzling Christmas lights. While it is a source of great joy to me, I cannot help, as I sit enchanted in front of it, also being reminded of a phrase that my father often used when I was a child. If I had left the lights on in my bedroom or on the landing, he would shout, 'Why doesn't anyone turn the lights off in this house? The place is lit up like a Christmas tree!' I would have been horrified if I had known that, 30 years later, I would be using the same phrase to my own children!

My use of the phrase does not solely reflect my concern for my electricity bills but is also the result of the environmental impact of wasting electricity. I have spent many an evening explaining to my children the virtues of reducing, reusing and recycling. Yet few of us are beyond reproach when it comes to our efforts to counter climate change. As I was brushing my teeth one day, my young daughter put me firmly in my place. She burst into the bathroom, stared at the sink and commented in a concerned voice, 'Look at God's tears running down the plug hole!' When I asked her what she meant, she answered, 'Every time you waste water, Daddy, God is crying.'

That incident brought it home to me that even those of us who deem ourselves to be environmentally engaged can always do more to counter the threat to our planet. If we search our actions and behaviour, we'll discover there is always something we can change or some way we can do that little bit more—reducing water wastage, recycling our refuse, reusing plastic bags, buying fruit and vegetables that are in season, choosing to walk or cycle rather than drive, sharing lifts with others, eating less meat, supporting environmental groups and charities, reducing our air miles and so on. But my daughter had also hit upon an important theological truth—that God truly cares about the world around us. After all, the most striking aspect of the covenant with Noah is that it is between God and 'all living creatures of every kind on the earth'. As if to hammer this home, that fact is mentioned five times in this short passage alone!

When we see a wonderful rainbow decorating our sky, we should be reminded not only of God's compassion for us, but also of his unceasing love for all of his creation. Noah and the nativity are inextricably linked, and both encourage us to make bold, practical moves to heal the brokenness of our fragile world. It should not be out of a sense of duty or obligation that we care for this magnificent world, but because of the rainbow and the incarnation. After all, when we recognise the person of Jesus in each and every part of God's wonderful creation, we will not be able to sit on our hands and do nothing as our planet suffers.

## Reflection

*Sit next to a Christmas tree and appreciate its beauty. As you contemplate the Christmas lights, consider what you personally can do to show your care, love and attention for our beautiful planet, and pray that God will inspire you to act.*

# 22–28 December

# Christ in our lives

Christmas Day is nearly upon us! But as we enjoy our festivities this year, we must not lose sight of the significance of the event we celebrate. We even base our calendar on the birth that happened in a rather obscure corner of the Roman empire. Time itself is split by the event, as evidenced by our use of the terms BC (before Christ) and AD (*anno Domini*, the year of our Lord). Following Neil Armstrong becoming the first human to walk on the moon in July 1969, President Richard Nixon made an announcement to a proud nation. 'Today', he said, 'is the greatest day since creation.' A friend of his, the evangelist Billy Graham, immediately took him to task, pointing out that the first Christmas Day was far more momentous!

Many of us eagerly look forward to Christmas Day and enjoy the celebrations. Often, however, its ultimate significance is downplayed. Rarely does it connect with the rest of the year, so its importance is seen as temporary and rooted simply in fleeting pleasure. In a promotional video for their internet podcast, which has been downloaded over 300 million times, the comedian Ricky Gervais and his friend Karl Pilkington discuss the festive season. Pilkington claims that the meaning of Christmas lies in the food, drink and parties. When Ricky Gervais challenges him and asks him about the nativity story, he dismisses the incarnation as having no contemporary significance: 'It's not important. It's *so* not important, this story. I don't need an old story… I could do without it. If someone said we're getting rid of it, I'd go, "All right."'

Yet the nativity is not simply an ancient story from a dusty old book. The incarnation is about experiencing Christ *now*. A wonderful consequence of the 'Word made flesh' is that Jesus is still involved in a dynamic relationship with the world. After all, God did not just reside in human form for a fleeting 33 years; he is still engaged in every part of our lives. If we open our eyes, ears and hearts, we will find that the Word is still becoming flesh today.

# Appreciating life

### Mark 10:13–16

People were bringing little children to Jesus for him to place his hands on them, but the disciples rebuked them. When Jesus saw this, he was indignant. He said to them, 'Let the little children come to me, and do not hinder them, for the kingdom of God belongs to such as these. Truly I tell you, anyone who will not receive the kingdom of God like a little child will never enter it.' And he took the children in his arms, placed his hands on them and blessed them.

From the moment I woke up last Christmas Eve I was rushing from one chore to the next. I felt like a little hamster on a treadmill, desperately trying to keep up with the pace of the festive rush. I wrapped all my presents before rushing out to post cards through friends' doors. I then raced to the supermarket to do a last-minute Christmas food shop. After sprinting around the store and throwing all manner of edible delights into my trolley, I stood in a huge queue at the tills for what seemed to be a lifetime. Finally, as I watched my groceries being scanned, I breathed a sigh of relief that I'd finally finished my chores—my wife would be so proud of me. It was only then it dawned on me that my wallet was at home on the kitchen table! As I tried to explain to the poor checkout assistant, some impatient customers in the long line behind me quickly lost their Christmas spirit. Then, from the corner of my eye, I noticed someone who was enjoying the whole ugly scene a bit too much: a young boy, lollipop in mouth, was looking over and giggling to himself.

Later that night, as I sat calmly in Midnight Mass, my embarrassment finally began to subside and I began to see the funny side of the situation. I started to think about what had happened, especially about the child who had found it all so amusing. The Welsh poet W.H. Davies' famous rhyme came to my mind: 'A poor life this if, full of care, we have no time to stop and stare.' In our passage today, Jesus tells us that we should become like children if we are to draw closer to God. By doing so, perhaps he was actually urging us to slow our lives down just a little and start to see them from a different perspective.

Young children often don't get caught up in the whirlwind of life. Instead, they seem to live in the moment, enjoying things here and now, with little concern for what has been or what is to come. I remember being in the town square of Maastricht in the Netherlands when a street performer was creating huge bubbles that would float past the crowd and then be taken heavenwards. My children were entranced at these seemingly magical bubbles, and I was heartened by their faces of awe and joy. As a character from the film *Knocked Up* (2007) put it: 'I wish I liked anything as much as my kids like bubbles; their smiling faces just point out our inability to enjoy anything!'

There's certainly a lesson here for us. The 2005 documentary film *Unknown White Male* tells the true tale of 37-year-old Doug Bruce, who one day found himself suffering from complete amnesia, forgetting every single thing about his past. It is fascinating to hear him describe the joy and wonder of discovering life again, as if for the first time. 'I would be aware of everything; everything would interest me;

everything was totally new,' he recalls. The simple pleasures in life became moments of grace: eating chocolate mousse and strawberries; listening to The Rolling Stones; visiting an art gallery; watching how people interacted with each other; and feeling the sand under his feet and the power of the waves as he visited the seaside. 'Doug now saw the world with the eyes of a newborn baby, but appreciated it with the mind of an adult,' explained the director Rupert Murray.

In our hectic lives, it's not easy to slow down the pace and truly enjoy the present moment, especially during the Christmas rush. In fact, it can sometimes seem impossible. But perhaps that makes it all the more important to find just five minutes every day when we put the brakes on life's roller coaster and take time for ourselves. By doing so, we, like Doug Bruce, start to see the world as a child does, but with the appreciation of an adult. After all, as Gandhi reminded us: 'There's more to life than increasing its speed.'

## Reflection

*Take some time for yourself today, even if it's just five minutes with a cup of tea. As best you can, try to lay aside any worries and concerns you have about preparation for Christmas and New Year, and ask God to open your eyes to the wonder of his creation over the festive period.*

# Laughter

### Isaiah 55:9–13

*'As the heavens are higher than the earth,*
  *so are my ways higher than your ways*
  *and my thoughts than your thoughts.*
*As the rain and the snow*
  *come down from heaven,*
*and do not return to it*
  *without watering the earth*
*and making it bud and flourish,*
  *so that it yields seed for the sower and bread for the*
  *eater,*
*so is my word that goes out from my mouth:*
  *it will not return to me empty,*
*but will accomplish what I desire*
  *and achieve the purpose for which I sent it.*
*You will go out in joy*
  *and be led forth in peace;*
*the mountains and hills*
  *will burst into song before you,*
*and all the trees of the field*
  *will clap their hands.*
*Instead of the thorn-bush will grow the juniper,*
  *and instead of briers the myrtle will grow.*
*This will be for the Lord's renown,*
  *for an everlasting sign,*
  *that will endure for ever.'*

My daughter has a CD of Bible stories that she puts on to help her get to sleep at night. One evening, after reading her bedtime story, I pressed play on her music system. 'No!' she snapped. 'I don't like track number one—put it straight to track two.' Inquisitive about this dislike of the first track, I asked about her problem. 'Well, I don't see what's special about healing ten frogs,' she explained in a matter-of-fact way, as if I would understand immediately. When she noticed the blank look on my face, she added, 'Actually, it might mean ten toads.' Still I was completely lost as to what she was talking about. 'Well, Daddy,' she continued to explain, 'it definitely describes Jesus healing ten leapers.' Her confusion between the words 'lepers' and 'leapers' made me burst out laughing, and helped sweeten the pill of the hard day's work from which I'd just returned.

Laughter is part and parcel of our lives, and it often breaks through into them, taking us by surprise and bringing much-needed relief, even at times of difficulty. Many of us regard the festive season as one of fun and laughter, and we even refer to 'Christmas cheer'. Those who seem grumpy or moody during this time are said to be the proverbial Scrooges, because they bring to mind the 'Bah! Humbug!' attitude of the protagonist of Charles Dickens's novel *A Christmas Carol* (1843). The fun of the festive parties, the cheer of the Christmas Day dinner table, the jokes in the crackers that we pull, the comedies that fill our televisions and the humour of the pantomimes and school plays all lead to the sound of laughter filling our world during Christmas time.

While most of us would agree that laughter is a wonderful gift from God, far too often we separate our sense of humour from our faith. Some of the services in our churches are so solemn and serious that it might seem to an outsider that the Christian faith is dark, depressing and dreary. Down the years many prominent church leaders have even ignored the fact that the Bible is infused with a zest and a joy for life. The early church father Jerome, for example, regarded laughter as 'a sign of ungodliness', claiming that it 'would be punished on the Day of Judgment'.

In the university theology course that I teach, I show the students a number of images from down the centuries and across the world, to facilitate discussion on how different cultures and different eras have viewed the person of Jesus Christ. Each year, the one picture that causes the most division of opinion is the *Laughing Jesus*, an anonymous 20th-century sketch of Jesus throwing his head back in hearty laughter. The image makes some students feel uncomfortable, as it is so far divorced from the traditional picture of a serious, solemn Jesus. Yet for many of my other students, the *Laughing Jesus* is a liberating picture, as it reveals something integral about the character of Jesus. Our saviour is not stern and judgmental, but joyful and loving, bringing hope, strength and inner healing into our lives, even when we are facing difficulties. As in our passage today, the Bible reassures us that our God is a colourful, joyous Father, rather than a drab, grey deity. The wonderful picture of the mountains bursting into song and the trees clapping their hands, as if they are characters in an uplifting musical, should bring smiles to our faces. It should help us remember that, while God did become flesh to show us that he understands what it is like to suffer, he also became flesh to affirm that he knows what it's like to laugh. As Martin Luther put it, 'If I am not allowed to laugh in heaven, I don't want to go there!'

## Reflection

*There are certain things that make each of us smile or laugh. It might be watching a DVD of a comedy series, or phoning a particular friend, or just spending some time remembering moments of joy and fun. Try to do something today that will lift your spirits, and, as you laugh or smile, thank God that he brings joy into our lives.*

# Music

**Psalm 150**

*Praise the Lord.*
*Praise God in his sanctuary;*
  *praise him in his mighty heavens.*
*Praise him for his acts of power;*
  *praise him for his surpassing greatness.*
*Praise him with the sounding of the trumpet,*
  *praise him with the harp and lyre,*
*praise him with tambourine and dancing,*
  *praise him with the strings and pipe,*
*praise him with the clash of cymbals,*
  *praise him with resounding cymbals.*

*Let everything that has breath praise the Lord.*
*Praise the Lord.*

Recently a friend sent me a link to a short film on a video-sharing website. Something intrigued me about the title of his message—'The Power of Music'—so I immediately viewed the video. It turned out to be an uplifting five-minute watch, which showed a true-life, secretly filmed 'flash mob': a large group of carol singers spread across a busy shopping arcade suddenly bursting into song. The faces of the shoppers change from confusion and disbelief to pure joy, as they realise that this spectacular show is being performed especially for them. By the time the group start singing 'Go tell it on the mountain', numerous onlookers have begun to join in, while others have started to clap their hands and dance!

There is something about music that lifts our spirits and touches our hearts. It is, therefore, perfectly natural that the Christian faith has such a close relationship with music. Many of us will have attended carol services over the Christmas period so far, while many seasonal pop hits, such as 'Mary's boy child' and 'When a child is born', are very much rooted in the incarnation. Whether it is Christmas or not, people of faith certainly find it natural to praise God through music. This is nothing new. Our passage today shows the enthusiasm with which the early Israelites used various instruments to worship their God. That our churches use a similarly wide range of instruments is testament to the continuing power of music in our lives. Praise him on the organ or the piano; praise him on the drums and guitar; praise him with worship leaders or gospel choirs; let everything that has breath praise the Lord!

It is certainly true that very few of us could say that we are unaffected by music, whether popular or classical. In fact, most of us would probably claim that, without music, something truly wonderful would be lacking from our lives. Music has a universal appeal. It can inspire our thoughts and emotions and bring joy into our lives. There is even much evidence of the great benefits of music therapy on both the young and the old. The documentary film *Alive Inside* (2013) describes how a nursing home for the elderly is transformed when the residents are given iPods to listen to the music that inspired them when they were younger. One resident, who is in such a state that he cannot even recognise his own daughter, is described as 'inert, maybe depressed, unresponsive and almost unalive'. The staff then play him the religious music of his youth. In front of our eyes, it is as if he becomes a different person altogether. His eyes light up, he sings along with the melodies, and, even after the headphones are removed, he speaks with passion, enthusiasm and energy. He even breaks off the interview to sing the Bing Crosby classic 'I'll be home for Christmas'. He finishes by explaining the importance of music to him: 'The Lord came to me and made me holy. I'm a holy man, so he gave me these sounds.'

Beautiful compositions can profoundly affect us in the deepest levels of our psyche, far beyond our thoughts or intellect, and in this way God touches us through the music to which we listen. As Christmas carols and songs play all around us, there can be no doubt that music seems to hold a power that points to something beyond our everyday experiences. Little wonder that it can inspire us, uplift us, soothe our worries and calm our anxieties. 'You know what music is?' asks Robin Williams's character in the film *August Rush* (2007). 'It's God's little reminder that there's something else besides us in this universe.'

## Reflection

*Put on some of your favourite music and simply sit, relax and enjoy God's wonderful gift of melody. As you listen, thank God that, just as he created us, so we also were given the gift of creativity. Thank him for the healing beauty of music and ask that he might touch and inspire you through the music you enjoy.*

# Memories

### Isaiah 9:2–7

*The people walking in darkness*
  *have seen a great light;*
*on those living in the land of deep darkness*
  *a light has dawned.*
*You have enlarged the nation*
  *and increased their joy;*
*they rejoice before you*
  *as people rejoice at the harvest,*
*as warriors rejoice*
  *when dividing the plunder.*
*For as in the day of Midian's defeat,*
  *you have shattered*
*the yoke that burdens them,*
  *the bar across their shoulders,*
  *the rod of their oppressor.*
*Every warrior's boot used in battle*
  *and every garment rolled in blood*
*will be destined for burning,*
  *will be fuel for the fire.*
*For to us a child is born,*
  *to us a son is given,*
  *and the government will be on his shoulders.*
*And he will be called*
  *Wonderful Counsellor, Mighty God,*
  *Everlasting Father, Prince of Peace.*

*Of the greatness of his government and peace*
   *there will be no end.*
*He will reign on David's throne*
   *and over his kingdom,*
*establishing and upholding it*
   *with justice and righteousness*
   *from that time on and for ever.*
*The zeal of the Lord Almighty*
   *will accomplish this.*

Our reading today looks forward to the first Christmas, when a child would be born to bring peace into our conflicts, hope into our despair and light into our darkness. Because of Jesus' life and death, this has become a present reality, but it is also a promise for our future. Because of what Jesus taught and accomplished, the future is bright, however hard our present moments may be. We look forward in hope to a time of peace, justice and righteousness, and we commit personally to helping him bring this into our everyday lives.

Rather than looking forward on Christmas Day, though, many of us find ourselves looking back, especially if we are missing a loved one. Again, our passage today gives us hope of light in our darkness. After all, our faith teaches us that when we love, we tread on divine ground. Thus our experiences of love are eternal and our memories of love go beyond the physical presence of people and places. Memories can bring us sadness, but, if we choose to allow them to, they can also bring us great joy. Whether we are remembering a person lost or a time long-gone, we can rejoice in the memories of happy times.

The 2010 Oscar-nominated documentary *Nostalgia for the Light* follows two groups of people in Chile. The first is a group of astronomers attempting to discover the origins of our solar system. The second is a group of women who still comb the Chilean deserts for the remains of loved ones who had disappeared during Pinochet's dictatorship. The film ends by asserting that, whoever we are and whatever we're doing, we should never underestimate the value and beauty of our memories. 'I am convinced that memory has a gravitational force,' the narrator concludes. 'It is constantly attracting us. Those who have a memory are able to live in the fragile present moment. Those who have none don't live anywhere.' In fact, the people of South America champion their memories to such an extent that they consider their lost ones still to be living in a very real way. In some Latin American churches, the community's roll-call also includes the deceased, with the congregation shouting out, '*El presente!*' ('Present!') as each person's name is read out, whether dead or alive.

We should value and appreciate our memories as gifts from the living God. They recreate events, people and places, and are able to lift our hearts and souls. It is natural that at Christmas we should look back to happy times, as well as looking forward to the hope of a future reunited with our loved ones. However, it is also important to appreciate Christ in the present moment, in the here and now. Recently I had a lovely email from a friend who mentioned how his life used to be a stream of fond memories of the past alongside intense worries for the future. He described how he gradually realised that, while it is good to live with one foot in the past and one foot in the future, we must never forget that our body is in the present. In *A Christmas Carol* by Charles Dickens, Scrooge is shown both the past and the future by ghostly apparitions. This occurs for one reason only—to bring more joy, hope and love to his present life. Both remembering and looking forward are important to our existence, but they only take on real meaning if we allow them to inform the present.

## Reflection

*On this Christmas Day, we remember that God sent his Son to bring light into our darkness. That light still shines in our lives— through our thoughts, our actions and our memories. Today, pledge that you do not allow these things to hold you back, but to bring hope and joy to the here and now. Ask God to especially allow your memories of those dear to you to inspire you to help bring his love into the world. Finally, ask God to help you enjoy today's celebrations, safe in the knowledge that by doing so, you are storing up further memories to hearten and inspire you in the future.*

# 26 December

# Food

## Ecclesiastes 8:15–17

So I commend the enjoyment of life, because there is nothing better for a person under the sun than to eat and drink and be glad. Then joy will accompany them in their toil all the days of the life God has given them under the sun.

When I applied my mind to know wisdom and to observe the labour that is done on earth – people getting no sleep day or night – then I saw all that God has done. No one can comprehend what goes on under the sun. Despite all their efforts to search it out, no one can discover its meaning. Even if the wise claim they know, they cannot really comprehend it.

## 1 Corinthians 10:31–33

Whether you eat or drink or whatever you do, do it all for the glory of God. Do not cause anyone to stumble, whether Jews, Greeks or the church of God – even as I try to please everyone in every way. For I am not seeking my own good but the good of many, so that they may be saved.

At the chaplaincy where I work, we have regular weekly events, discussing how our faith relates to topics as wide-ranging as the arts, health, politics and poetry. Once a term, we break from the usual educational format to celebrate a festival that we have invented. We call it 'World Food Night'. On that evening, we invite our students to bring in a dish from their home country for us all to share. We are treated to a veritable feast, with tasty delights from as far away as

China, India, the Caribbean, Africa and the United States, as well as from countries closer to home such as Germany, France and Italy. While this event is meant to give relief from the academic discussions, the food actually facilitates some wonderful conversations among the students, and they sit and chat for hours, sharing stories, thoughts and ideas.

We can often be in a real rush to eat our food. As a society, we may be spending more and more time watching cookery programmes and buying books written by famous chefs, but we are also falling into bad dining habits—eating on the go between meetings at work, making use of fast-food outlets and eating pre-prepared meals as we sit and watch TV. Still, Christmas is an occasion when many of us do take time to prepare food, and we will often delight in the company of friends and family as we eat together.

Our passages today give some indication that this is exactly what God was expecting us to do when he gave us the gift of food. It is clear from the Gospel stories that Jesus saw food as an important part of life. He ate and drank at meals and parties; he defended his disciples when they picked and ate grain on the Sabbath; he and his friends ate a final, significant meal before his death; and he even shared food with his disciples after his resurrection. Subsequently, food has been seen as something that should be savoured and appreciated as a key part of our faith. From the bread and wine at our Communion table to the tasty delights at our various festivals (mince pies, Christmas puddings, pancakes, Easter eggs and so on), food is regarded as something that brings people together and helps nurture relationships.

When I was a child, my dad used to take us to eat at the local monastery. My elder brother and I christened those visits our 'meals with the monks'. I must admit that I did not particularly enjoy the food, as the cook would put onions with everything—an eight-year-old's nightmare! But a Communion service would always follow the onion torture, and I remember being struck by the fact that, for this group of monks, the Communion table and the dinner table were very much part of the same world. At both tables, there was the same attitude of unity, love and respect between those sharing the meals. Perhaps this truly reflected the original Last Supper, which, after all, was very much a meal between friends. The New Testament informs us that a joyous meal continued to be the normal setting in which the early Christians met together for fellowship and worship (Acts 2:46), and this meal was so rooted in friendship and harmony that it was known as the 'love (*agape*) feast'.

As we reflect on the wonderful meals we are eating over the festive period, we are reminded that food is one of God's gifts to us, and it can nourish both our faith and our bodies. If we allow it to, it can also help strengthen our family bonds, our work relationships and our friendships. Perhaps the Greek philosopher Epicurus was not so far from the truth when he remarked that 'even before we look for something to eat, we should look for someone to eat with'.

## Reflection

*Really enjoy your food today. If you can, linger over the preparation of your meals, noticing the colours and smells of all the ingredients, then savour every bite you take as you eat. Thank God for the gift of food. In a prayer, commit to using as many mealtimes as you can, at home or in work, to nurture your relationships—with family, friends, colleagues, acquaintances or lonely neighbours!*

# Film

## Matthew 2:1–12

After Jesus was born in Bethlehem in Judea, during the time of King Herod, Magi from the east came to Jerusalem and asked, 'Where is the one who has been born king of the Jews? We saw his star when it rose and have come to worship him.'

When King Herod heard this he was disturbed, and all Jerusalem with him. When he had called together all the people's chief priests and teachers of the law, he asked them where the Messiah was to be born. 'In Bethlehem in Judea,' they replied, 'for this is what the prophet has written:

'"But you, Bethlehem, in the land of Judah,
  are by no means least among the rulers of Judah;
 for out of you will come a ruler
  who will shepherd my people Israel."'

Then Herod called the Magi secretly and found out from them the exact time the star had appeared. He sent them to Bethlehem and said, 'Go and search carefully for the child. As soon as you find him, report to me, so that I too may go and worship him.'

After they had heard the king, they went on their way, and the star they had seen when it rose went ahead of them until it stopped over the place where the child was. When they saw the star, they were overjoyed. On coming to the house, they saw the child with his mother Mary, and they bowed down and worshipped him. Then they opened their treasures and presented him with gifts of gold, frankincense and myrrh. And having been warned in a dream not to go back to Herod, they returned to their country by another route.

Stories are important in scripture, from the wonderful narratives of the book of Genesis (Noah's ark, Joseph and his colourful coat and so on) to Jesus' intriguing and enlightening parables. Such tales continue to inspire children and adults alike. While the birth of Christ, the coming of God made flesh, has profound implications for our lives, there is no escaping the fact that it is also a riveting story. Our passage today, the story of the Wise Men, is part of this great narrative. As a child, this episode was so magical that I was desperate to be one of the three kings in our nativity plays at school. The story of their long journey to find a wealthy king, bearing precious gifts to give him, only to find that this king was born in the dirt and squalor of a stable, thrilled and inspired me.

In later life, my love of stories led me to become a film fanatic, and I have proudly passed this enthusiasm for movies on to my son. We even have a party trick, in which we ask people to name films and he rattles off all the principal actors. This year he even persuaded me to stay up and watch the Oscars. We lounged on the sofas, munching popcorn, until the early hours of the morning. Spare a thought for my poor students, though, as I was lecturing them at 10am the next morning. I don't think I made much sense after only four hours of sleep!

I sometimes wonder why so many of us are drawn towards film. There are certain dangers inherent in this medium, as particular movies can assert negative influences on us, but others can actually affect us in a profoundly spiritual way. Mark Kermode, one of Britain's foremost film critics, writes that cinema itself is 'a sacred space, as hallowed as a church'. Films certainly work alongside our faith to teach us something about the ultimate questions of life and death, and they especially give insights into our relationships with one another. The ancient Greeks would attend their theatres on festival days. They would laugh out loud and cheer at the comedies and literally cry together at the tragedies. It was believed that attendance at these performances was essential in strengthening their bonds with each other and to reassure each and every person that they were not alone in any pain or trouble they were going through.

Modern-day films allow us to do exactly that. They can encourage our children to stand alongside heroes as diverse as Buzz Lightyear, Shrek and Harry Potter, and by doing so, to learn the true meaning of friendship, sacrifice and love. Likewise, the most popular films for adults are the ones where we learn about love and compassion through people who, like us, face all sorts of adversities. In this sense, films are not just about entertaining us for a couple of hours. Rather, like the Christmas story itself, they inspire us to stand alongside and share the struggles of the people in our lives—lonely relatives, elderly neighbours, friends in need or strangers in the street. After all, the best films capture both our imaginations and our hearts, so let's not leave them in the dark of the cinema or boxed up in our televisions!

## Reflection
*Christmas is a time when blockbusters are released in the cinemas and our television channels are full of great films. Watch a good film this evening. It might be one on the TV or a*

DVD. If you haven't got time to watch a whole film, watch part of one or a TV drama or even a soap opera. Relax and silently thank God for the gift of cinema and television.

# 28 December

# Friends

**Mark 2:1–11**

A few days later, when Jesus again entered Capernaum, the people heard that he had come home. They gathered in such large numbers that there was no room left, not even outside the door, and he preached the word to them. Some men came, bringing to him a paralysed man, carried by four of them. Since they could not get him to Jesus because of the crowd, they made an opening in the roof above Jesus by digging through it and then lowered the mat the man was lying on. When Jesus saw their faith, he said to the paralysed man, 'Son, your sins are forgiven.'

Now some teachers of the law were sitting there, thinking to themselves, 'Why does this fellow talk like that? He's blaspheming! Who can forgive sins but God alone?'

Immediately Jesus knew in his spirit that this was what they were thinking in their hearts, and he said to them, 'Why are you thinking these things? Which is easier: to say to this paralysed man, "Your sins are forgiven," or to say, "Get up, take your mat and walk"? But I want you to know that the Son of Man has authority on earth to forgive sins.' So he said to the man, 'I tell you, get up, take your mat and go home.'

Friendship is one of the most wonderful gifts in our lives. Over Christmas, most of us will delight in meeting up with our friends over drinks or food, sharing stories and laughing together. One of the things I like most about today's passage is the integral role played in the incident by a group of unnamed friends. In fact, the healing itself would never have taken place without these friends. They were the ones who carried the paralysed man to Jesus; they were the ones who struggled to get him to the top of the roof; they were the ones who had the vision to make a hole in the roof and lower him down. Without them, we have no story; without them, we have no miracle!

Recently, an article in a film magazine got me thinking further about the importance of friends. The article, entitled 'The 50 Coolest Movie Friendships', analysed the most inspirational friendships in films down the years. One of the featured relationships that caught my attention was the friendship of the two hobbits in The Lord of the Rings trilogy (2001–2003). Frodo and Sam's rapport deepens as they travel for many miles to reach Mount Doom, where Frodo has to discard the powerful and malevolent ring. In The Return of the King Frodo collapses with exhaustion at the foot of the mountain and cannot physically continue. His friend kneels beside him and encourages him by recounting beautiful images of their homeland. With tears in his eyes, Sam finishes his rousing words by lifting up his fallen comrade and carrying him up the mountain. 'I can't carry [the ring] for you,' he says, 'but I can carry you!'

The touching and inspiring friendship of Frodo and Sam is certainly one reason why both the original books by J.R.R. Tolkien and the films have proved so popular down the years. It is not inconceivable that Tolkien, a devout Christian, had Matthew 11:28–30 in mind as he wrote the Mount Doom episode. In that passage, Jesus urged his disciples to lay their burdens and worries on him. The Bible certainly reveals Jesus to be a good friend to those around him. He was with his family and friends in times of celebration, and he supported them through times of difficulty and sadness.

This is a good model for our own friendships. As an old German proverb puts it, 'A sorrow shared is a sorrow halved; a joy shared is a joy doubled.' Life is not about choosing friends who will be good to us, but it's about doing everything we can to be a good friend ourselves. If we know a friend is lonely, we can phone or visit them. If a friend is ill, we can cook a meal or go shopping for them. Christmas is a time when we need to appreciate and thank God for the people around us, and what better way to do this than showing ourselves to be loving and caring companions, especially to those who most need our company and support.

## Reflection
*Think of a friend who is in need at the moment. Perhaps they are lonely, ill or grieving the loss of a loved one. Pray for them, asking God to bring them peace and comfort. After praying, do something practical to help that friend. Maybe you could phone them for a chat or visit them in person (or pledge to visit them soon). If you do visit them, why not take them a small gift to show that you appreciate their company, or, if they are elderly or infirm, you could carry out some little act of help for them, such as going shopping or cooking a meal for them.*

# 29 December–4 January

# Being Christ in the world

A few years ago I was walking down the Champs-Élysées in Paris when I was approached by a smartly dressed young man who offered to sketch my portrait for me. After a moment of hesitation, my vanity got the better of me and I enthusiastically agreed to his offer. 'An up-and-coming young French painter,' I thought to myself. 'This could be worth a fortune in the future!' So I sat patiently on a small stool for what seemed like a lifetime, as he diligently sketched behind his easel. Imagine my shock and horror when he finally turned the paper around and there was a picture of me with huge flapping ears, big chubby cheeks and a long Cyrano-de-Bergerac-style nose! I still blame the whole experience on my low GCSE grade in French. After all, it was my poor French vocabulary that had led to the confusion—he had actually been a caricaturist, not a portrait artist!

Caricatures do give us some hint of what people really look like and how they act, but they exaggerate certain features of their appearance and personality and ignore others. The baby Jesus is not a caricature, but it's still very easy for us to forget that we only get a hint of who Jesus was from this little baby. The nativity story can certainly be presented as quaint and sweet, but, like a caricature, it only hints at the full picture of the incarnation. In the comedy film *Talladega Nights: The Ballad of Ricky Bobby* (2006), stock-car-racing legend Ricky Bobby prays his mealtime grace to 'Lord baby Jesus', who does not 'even know a word yet' and is 'just a little infant and so cuddly'. When his wife reminds him, 'Sweetie, Jesus did grow up,' Ricky Bobby replies, 'Well, look, I like the Christmas Jesus best.' As we slowly leave our Christmas celebrations behind, we remember that Jesus did indeed grow up, and, through his saving work and radical teaching, he now offers us love, peace, hope and joy. He also urges us to model ourselves on him and so to share that love, peace, hope and joy with others too, whoever they are and whatever their backgrounds.

# Bringing Christ to earth

## Luke 14:12–24

Jesus said to his host, 'When you give a luncheon or dinner, do not invite your friends, your brothers or sisters, your relatives, or your rich neighbours; if you do, they may invite you back and so you will be repaid. But when you give a banquet, invite the poor, the crippled, the lame, the blind, and you will be blessed. Although they cannot repay you, you will be repaid at the resurrection of the righteous.'

When one of those at the table with him heard this, he said to Jesus, 'Blessed is the one who will eat at the feast in the kingdom of God.'

Jesus replied: 'A certain man was preparing a great banquet and invited many guests. At the time of the banquet he sent his servant to tell those who had been invited, "Come, for everything is now ready."

'But they all alike began to make excuses. The first said, "I have just bought a field, and I must go and see it. Please excuse me."

'Another said, "I have just bought five yoke of oxen, and I'm on my way to try them out. Please excuse me."

'Still another said, "I have just got married, so I can't come."

'The servant came back and reported this to his master. Then the owner of the house became angry and ordered his servant, "Go out quickly into the streets and alleys of the town and bring in the poor, the crippled, the blind and the lame."

'"Sir," the servant said, "what you ordered has been done, but there is still room."

'Then the master told his servant, "Go out to the roads and country lanes and compel them to come in, so that my house will be full. I tell you, not one of those who were invited will get a taste of my banquet."'

Working as a chaplain at Cardiff University has many joys. If someone were to ask me to choose the highlight of the year, however, the decision would not be hard. Wales is a nation that is immensely proud of its language, traditions and culture as being very distinct from those of the rest of the United Kingdom. Each year at the chaplaincy we celebrate Wales's national day, St David's Day, with a service of Welsh readings, poems and hymns, not least that most famous of Welsh hymns, '*Arglwydd, Arwain Trwy'r Anialwch*', sung worldwide as 'Guide me, O thou great Jehovah'. When our voices are finally hoarse, the service comes to an end and we devour copious amounts of traditional Welsh fare: leek soup, Welsh cakes and *bara-brith* or raisin loaf. The 'great banquet' is always packed to the rafters, with students from all nations and different backgrounds joining together to show their appreciation for the country in which they are residing.

St David's Day is on the first day of March as the great Welsh saint is believed to have died on that day, way back in the sixth century. His last words were reported to have been, '*Cofiwch y pethau bychain.*' ('Remember the small things.') Well, that's easy for him to say! But it's not so easy for us to put into practice in our own hectic 21st-century lives. As we face the hustle and bustle of the post-Christmas sales in our shopping centres, and as we prepare to return to our places of work, where deadlines and targets are the order of the day, we should remind ourselves that this little bit of advice is as important today as it was almost 1500 years ago.

St David was part of the Celtic tradition, which recognised God in even the smallest details of life. This community believed that the picture of the great banquet in today's parable was not just an image for the next world. Our own world can be a place of joy, peace and love if we strive to connect with God in our daily lives. The Celtic Christians did not believe that God demanded a special effort from them in order to connect with him. Instead, they met him every day—in creation, in people, in places.

There's nothing unusual in this belief. Judaism, Christianity and Islam all emphasise that God's creation is essentially good, even the seemingly insignificant things. With so much suffering and pain in the world, we can easily forget that it is often the little things that make our lives interesting, meaningful and worthwhile: a beautiful sunset; laughing over coffee with a friend or family member; walking the dog in the park. Even something as simple as a smile from a stranger that we pass on the street can bring us joy. Whether we're Welsh or not, St David's final words can inspire us. So, in the busy-ness of our everyday lives, why don't we try to take some time out today, just to appreciate and savour those brief moments that bring joy and meaning to our lives—to 'remember the small things'.

## Reflection

*'So many people walk around with a meaningless life. They seem half-asleep, even when they're busy doing things they think are important. This is because they're chasing the wrong things'* (Morrie Schwartz, whose struggle with motor neurone disease is related in Mitch Albom's bestselling book Tuesdays with Morrie).

*Consider this quotation. How often are you so busy doing things you think are important that you miss the 'small things' that St David urged us to appreciate?*

# Our gifts and talents

### Matthew 25:14–29

'[The kingdom of heaven] will be like a man going on a journey, who called his servants and entrusted his wealth to them. To one he gave five bags of gold, to another two bags, and to another one bag, each according to his ability. Then he went on his journey. The man who had received five bags of gold went at once and put his money to work and gained five bags more. So also, the one with two bags of gold gained two more. But the man who had received one bag went off, dug a hole in the ground and hid his master's money.

'After a long time the master of those servants returned and settled accounts with them. The man who had received five bags of gold brought the other five. "Master," he said, "you entrusted me with five bags of gold. See, I have gained five more."

'His master replied, "Well done, good and faithful servant! You have been faithful with a few things; I will put you in charge of many things. Come and share your master's happiness!"

'The man with two bags of gold also came. "Master," he said, "you entrusted me with two bags of gold: see, I have gained two more."

'His master replied, "Well done, good and faithful servant! You have been faithful with a few things; I will put you in charge of many things. Come and share your master's happiness!"

'Then the man who had received one bag of gold came. "Master," he said, "I knew that you are a hard man, harvesting where you have not sown and gathering where you have not scattered seed. So I was afraid and went out and hid your gold in the ground. See, here is what belongs to you."

'His master replied, "You wicked, lazy servant! So you knew that I harvest where I have not sown and gather where I have not scattered seed? Well then, you should have put my money on deposit with the bankers, so that when I returned I would have received it back with interest.

'"So take the bag of gold from him and give it to the one who has ten bags. For whoever has will be given more, and they will have an abundance. Whoever does not have, even what they have will be taken from them."'

When I was younger I thought today's passage was a rather harsh parable. The poor servant, who had only been given one bag of gold in the first place, had not been wasteful or frivolous, but had simply not been forward-thinking enough to use what had been given to him wisely. For that, he had been chastised by his master as a wicked and lazy servant, and the little gold he had was taken away from him! However, this is not a parable about economics or how useful banks are. Rather, it is an important lesson for us about the God-given gifts with which we have all been blessed.

Not so long ago, I saw a report about a team of climbers from Anglesey in North Wales who became the first British people in 30 years to scale the summit of Afghanistan's highest mountain. The great mountains of my own Welsh homeland are dwarfed by the giant Afghan peak, which is over seven times higher than Snowdon! The report especially resonated with me as my father was brought up on the Isle of Anglesey and my home town of Penmaenmawr looks out over the Menai Straits, which divide Anglesey from the mainland. This brave and gifted group of climbers had even run out of food during the climb, but their skill and talent led to eventual success.

As someone who gets vertigo while changing light bulbs, I marvel at the achievement of my compatriots. It makes my own moderate gifts feel rather inadequate. But we should certainly not get disheartened when we reflect on our own inabilities or weaknesses. Instead, we should remember that each of us has various God-given gifts. The important thing, Jesus suggests in the parable, is not how impressive they are but what we do with them. I remember an advert some time back for the armed forces, which asked who the most important person in the army was. Was it the General? Or the soldier? Or the engineer? Or the cook? The answer was that they were all important, as they all worked for the good of each other. And isn't that the same in life generally? Sometimes our talents are obvious for everyone to see. We might be a great singer, or have the 'gift of the gab'. But sometimes they're less obvious. We might have a smile that can melt even the hardest heart; we might cheer up a room with our jokes; or we might simply have the gift of knowing when a friend needs a word of encouragement. Someone once said to me that 'a satsuma is not a failed orange'! In other words, all our talents are important, which is why it's helpful for us to take time to consider what our particular gifts are. We can then concentrate on how we use them in our everyday lives—and what better way to use them than to bring hope, happiness and love to the people around us?

## Reflection
*What talents and gifts have you been blessed with? If you are not sure, ask your partner or a friend about what they see as*

*your greatest gifts; sometimes other people see our talents better than we ourselves do. Try to use your particular gift today to help somebody, or to bring joy into somebody's life.*

# Being a saint

### Revelation 7:9–12

I looked, and there before me was a great multitude that no one could count, from every nation, tribe, people and language, standing before the throne and before the Lamb. They were wearing white robes and were holding palm branches in their hands. And they cried out in a loud voice:

*'Salvation belongs to our God,*
*who sits on the throne,*
*and to the Lamb.'*

All the angels were standing round the throne and round the elders and the four living creatures. They fell down on their faces before the throne and worshipped God, saying:

*'Amen!*
*Praise and glory*
*and wisdom and thanks and honour*
*and power and strength*
*be to our God for ever and ever.*
*Amen!'*

I was due to be born on 1 November, which is All Saints' Day in the Western liturgical calendar. My mum was excited about giving birth to her own personal saint. In the week running up to the day, she did everything she could to induce labour—from rough country drives to long mountain walks. On the night before All Saints' Day, she even fell for the old wives' tale of consuming a large dose of castor oil. Unfortunately, I didn't appear, and all that happened was that she spent the next few days on the toilet! In fact, it took another whole week for me to appear. When I arrived in the world, my father informed my mum that she really did have her own little saint, as 8 November is, in fact, All Saints of Wales Day! However, my behaviour over the next 18 years quickly dispelled the saintly hopes she had. 'Perhaps it would be more appropriate if you'd been born on Hallowe'en,' I recall her once teasing me.

Once, on my birthday, I was invited to a local church to be quizzed by a large group of teenagers about my work as a university chaplain. Three other people had also been invited—a local teacher, someone who worked with the homeless in the city and someone who worked for the Samaritans. All evening we were grilled by these inquisitive youngsters, and I answered questions as diverse as 'Why do you do what you do?', 'What is the meaning of life?' and, more popular than you might think, 'How much do you get paid?' When I was first approached to attend this evening I naturally enquired why I was being asked to give up my birthday. The vicar organising the event informed me that it was to commemorate All Saints of Wales Day, and they were asking a number of modern-day saints of Wales. I nearly fell off my chair laughing when I realised I was to represent a 'modern-day saint'. Yes, I do my best to help other people, but I'm certainly no St Francis or Mother Teresa!

After thinking about it for a while, though, I soon realised that my reaction revealed my own prejudices about what a saint actually was. I've always pictured saints as very holy people, with smiling faces, often immortalised in stained-glass windows, with little birds landing on their shoulders and halos over their heads. In some ways, our reading from the book of Revelation might allow such a misunderstanding, as this godly group wear white robes and hold palm branches in their hands. However, seen in the context of the rest of the Bible, this view of sainthood is challenged. Both Luke, the writer of Acts, and the apostle Paul paint a much more human and down-to-earth portrait of sainthood, referring to the early Christians in Jerusalem and elsewhere as 'saints' (see Acts 9:13, 32; Philippians 4:21, NIV 1984). Even today's reading reveals that saints are 'a great multitude from every nation, tribe, people and language'.

There is nothing super-human about sainthood, and thus we are all called to be saints. As Mother Teresa herself once said, each one of us has the ability to become 'pencils in the hand of God'. Sometimes it's clear that our actions are worthwhile—just think of the selfless work of hospital staff, carers, the emergency services and so on. Sometimes, though, actions such as visiting a lonely relative, or taking time to listen to a friend in need, or simply smiling and saying, 'Hello!' to our neighbours might seem insignificant to us. Often we're so hung up about our failings we forget that all our seemingly minor saintly actions bring much light and love to the world around us. As Albert Schweitzer, a former Nobel Peace Prize winner, once said, 'We certainly don't have to be angels to be saints.'

## Reflection

*The time has come to start thinking about New Year's resolutions! Perhaps this year it needn't be grand gestures that are forgotten by the end of January. Pause today to think of some realistic, saintly action that you will be able to carry out regularly, such as visiting an elderly neighbour, volunteering at a charity or a church, or actively caring for your local environment by, for example, clearing the litter. From tomorrow, make it your aim to become a pencil in the hand of God.*

# 1 January

# Ordinary people

## Luke 5:1–11

One day as Jesus was standing by the Lake of Gennesaret, the people were crowding round him and listening to the word of God. He saw at the water's edge two boats, left there by the fishermen, who were washing their nets. He got into one of the boats, the one belonging to Simon, and asked him to put out a little from the shore. Then he sat down and taught the people from the boat.

When he had finished speaking, he said to Simon, 'Put out into deep water, and let down the nets for a catch.'

Simon answered, 'Master, we've worked hard all night and haven't caught anything. But because you say so, I will let down the nets.'

When they had done so, they caught such a large number of fish that their nets began to break. So they signalled to their partners in the other boat to come and help them, and they came and filled both boats so full that they began to sink.

When Simon Peter saw this, he fell at Jesus' knees and said, 'Go away from me, Lord; I am a sinful man!' For he and all his companions were astonished at the catch of fish they had taken, and so were James and John, the sons of Zebedee, Simon's partners.

Then Jesus said to Simon, 'Don't be afraid; from now on you will fish for people.' So they pulled their boats up on shore, left everything and followed him.

For over a decade now, reality TV has been a mainstay in the corners of our living rooms. From the moment *Big Brother* hit our screens, with infamous characters such as Nasty Nick and Jade Goody, many of us became addicted to this form of television. These days, the most popular reality shows seem to be based around an interesting difference. On the one hand, there are programmes such as *Strictly Come Dancing* or *I'm a Celebrity, Get Me Out of Here* that take famous people and challenge them to try their hand at something for which they are not famous. On the other hand, there are programmes such as *The X Factor* or *Britain's Got Talent* that take so-called ordinary people and challenge them to use their talents to become famous. On these shows, we see people who will do almost anything to achieve fame. It seems our society is becoming more and more aware of this differentiation: there are the rich and famous and then there are the 'ordinary'. The desire for attention and wealth is so ingrained in us that, a few years back, a Channel 4 programme entitled *Space Cadets* saw a group of fame-seekers allowing themselves to be duped into believing they had been sent into space. It was only when they 'landed' back on earth and got out of the fake shuttle that it was revealed to them that the whole thing had been a set-up!

What is striking about stories in the Bible is that often the heroes are not famous or wealthy people. Rarely are they kings, emperors, entertainers or even soldiers. In today's reading we see the calling of three of Jesus' disciples—Peter, James and John. These were ordinary fisherman who became extraordinary men of God. In the same way, the people in the stable at the nativity weren't the famous, respected people of the ancient world. Luke's Gospel describes those present at

Jesus' manger—a group of poor, hired shepherds, who were given little respect socially, alongside his parents, Mary and Joseph, two unknown Jewish people. Matthew adds a group of travelling foreigners, the wise men, who arrive later on the scene.

Our Bible, not least the Christmas story, teaches us that there are no 'ordinary' people in God's eyes. He does not dwell on what we do, but sees our worth and value beyond our actions. He even sent his Son to show us the infinite extent of his love for each and every one of us—not just the rich, the powerful and the famous, but also the poor, the ill, the depressed, the asylum seekers, the drug-addicted, the alcoholics, the lonely and the homeless. This is the good news of the stable in Bethlehem. In God's eyes, all of us are truly precious. In God's eyes, all of us have the X factor.

## Reflection
*Today, each time you meet someone or talk to someone, try not to judge them or weigh them up in earthly terms, but remind yourself how important they are in God's eyes, and how much God loves them. Only then will you not be blinded by what they do, and only then can you truly appreciate who they are.*

# Being called

## 1 Samuel 3:3–10

The lamp of God had not yet gone out, and Samuel was lying down in the house of the Lord, where the ark of God was. Then the Lord called Samuel.

Samuel answered, 'Here I am.' And he ran to Eli and said, 'Here I am; you called me.'

But Eli said, 'I did not call; go back and lie down.' So he went and lay down.

Again the Lord called, 'Samuel!' And Samuel got up and went to Eli and said, 'Here I am; you called me.'

'My son,' Eli said, 'I did not call; go back and lie down.'

Now Samuel did not yet know the Lord: the word of the Lord had not yet been revealed to him.

A third time the Lord called, 'Samuel!' And Samuel got up and went to Eli and said, 'Here I am; you called me.'

Then Eli realised that the Lord was calling the boy. So Eli told Samuel, 'Go and lie down, and if he calls you, say, "Speak, Lord, for your servant is listening."' So Samuel went and lay down in his place.

The Lord came and stood there, calling as at the other times, 'Samuel! Samuel!'

Then Samuel said, 'Speak, for your servant is listening.'

Today's Old Testament reading is one of my favourite stories. I loved it so much when I was a child that I used to lie awake at night, straining to hear my name being called out. Each night, however, I was disappointed by the silence. Then one night I finally heard my name being called, like a whisper in the wind—'Trystan'. I thought my ears were deceiving me, but then I heard it again—'Trystan'. I remember being scared about talking directly to God, but I was also excited, because I'd read the story of Eli and Samuel and I knew what to do. I therefore replied confidently, 'Speak, Lord; your servant is listening.' And the voice replied, 'Good, Trystan, because I have such an important task for you—tomorrow you must go out and buy your wonderful older brother the most expensive birthday present you can find him!' At that point I noticed the shadow of my brother outside my door. I was distraught! I was actually so disappointed that, at that point, I came to the conclusion that God would never call someone like me. He only calls special people, I thought; he only calls great prophets, very holy people, good people, worthy people.

In fact most of our biblical heroes were far from perfect. Noah was fond of alcohol; Jacob was a deceitful cheat; David was an adulterer, who would have fitted very well into *Coronation Street* or *EastEnders*; Jonah was a coward; Peter was a violent hothead; and I could go on! God calls *all* of us, whoever we are, whatever we've done, however we act. After all, each and every one of us is a mixture of good and bad. Each of us has various God-given talents and gifts, but each of us also has a rebellious side, which is selfish and self-centred. As the theologian Hans Küng put it, 'Some of us are black sheep, some of us are white sheep, but the majority of us are simply zebras!'

Arthur Miller, in the play *Death of a Salesman* (1949), refers to the main protagonist, Willy Loman, as 'the saddest, self-centredest soul'. Here Miller stumbles across an important

Christian belief—that we are, indeed, all selfish, self-centred souls. That's the bad news, but there is also good news. The good news is that God loves us all, whatever our faults. Despite our weaknesses and even in our darkest moments, he uses each of us for his purpose. 'Oh here in dust and dirt, O here; the lilies of his love appear,' wrote the 17th-century Welsh poet Henry Vaughan.

For most of us, though, God will not appear in some supernatural way. Your own call might come through a friend suggesting you do something, or through a nagging feeling you've got, or through a flash of inspiration as you're soaking in the bath—a 'eureka' moment. *How* the call comes is not important. More important is that we hold on to the fact that God *is* calling us to use whatever gifts and talents we have to carry out his two key commandments—to love him and to love each other. In every part of our lives, we must learn to expect God, opening our eyes to his presence, our hearts to his love and our ears to his call. After all, the question is not '*Is* God calling you to do something?' Rather, the question is '*What* is God calling you to do?'

## Reflection

*Stop to think how you are being called to use your gifts and talents for God's glory. How can you use them to help others, to help your church or to bring light into people's lives? 'Oh here in dust and dirt, O here; the lilies of his love appear.'*

# Back to work

### Daniel 1:3–6, 17–20

Then the king ordered Ashpenaz, chief of his court officials, to bring into the king's service some of the Israelites from the royal family and the nobility—young men without any physical defect, handsome, showing aptitude for every kind of learning, well informed, quick to understand, and qualified to serve in the king's palace. He was to teach them the language and literature of the Babylonians. The king assigned them a daily amount of food and wine from the king's table. They were to be trained for three years, and after that they were to enter the king's service.

Among those who were chosen were some from Judah: Daniel, Hananiah, Mishael and Azariah...

To these four young men God gave knowledge and understanding of all kinds of literature and learning. And Daniel could understand visions and dreams of all kinds.

At the end of the time set by the king to bring them into his service, the chief official presented them to Nebuchadnezzar. The king talked with them, and he found none equal to Daniel, Hananiah, Mishael and Azariah; so they entered the king's service. In every matter of wisdom and understanding about which the king questioned them, he found them ten times better than all the magicians and enchanters in his whole kingdom.

In the chaplaincy where I work, I meet students who are studying an amazing range of subjects, from Norse poetry to neuroscience. One of the most frequent discussions is about who has the most lecture hours in the week and who is lucky enough to have the least. When the complaints start about the amount of lectures they have to attend, I remind them to be grateful that they are not Olympic swimmers. I once read an interview with Michael Phelps, the most decorated Olympian of all time, about his training for the Games. Each week he swam over 50 miles and spent hours in the gym. He had at least two massages and four ice baths daily to help his body to recover from the training. Even on Christmas Day he would do a full quota of training. The rest of the time he had to compensate for the calories he burnt off during training by consuming as much food as possible. An average man only needs 2,000 calories a day; Phelps consumed a staggering 12,000 calories! His breakfast alone consisted of a few rounds of toast, two cups of coffee, an omelette, a large bowl of porridge, three pancakes and three fried-egg sandwiches topped with cheese, lettuce, tomatoes, fried onions and mayonnaise!

Very few of us are Olympic athletes, but most of us work hard at what we do, and after our New Year break many of us will be going back to work today. Ecclesiastes 3:1–8 tells us that there's a time for everything: we might say there's a time for work, and a time for play; a time for study, and a time for rest. Now is the time for work, and we certainly need to take our work and study seriously. Rick Warren in *The Purpose Driven Life* wrote that 'work becomes worship when you dedicate it to God and perform it with an awareness of his presence'. Today's reading from Daniel shows us that Daniel and his friends did exactly that—they regarded their work and education as part of their duty to their creator. This can speak to us all, whether we are office workers, students, pastors, teachers, bankers, builders, shop assistants or stay-at-home parents. We must not forget that every part of our lives really matters to God and is, therefore, sacred.

God should be woven into every aspect of our lives. It's important that we don't leave Christ in the cradle as we leave this Christmas season behind. We must recognise him in every part of our lives—in our work, our study, our conversations with friends, our sport and our social lives. The people who love us—our friends, parents, husbands and wives—are genuinely interested in the whole of our lives, not just the exciting and fun parts. How much more, then, does our loving God want to be involved in every part of our lives—not just the play, but also the work!

## Reflection

*It's a good little exercise for us to try consciously to think of Christ walking alongside us as we go about our everyday lives. Sometimes we may feel unappreciated in our work, so it's a huge relief to remind ourselves that Christ is with us, and that he appreciates and cares about our work. Contemplate these words from Psalm 139:1–3 and 10:*

*You have searched me, Lord,*
*   and you know me.*
*You know when I sit and when I rise;*
*   you perceive my thoughts from afar.*
*You discern my going out and my lying down;*
*   you are familiar with all my ways...*
*your hand will guide me,*
*   your right hand will hold me fast.*

# Struggle

**Genesis 32:24–30**

So Jacob was left alone, and a man wrestled with him till daybreak. When the man saw that he could not overpower him, he touched the socket of Jacob's hip so that his hip was wrenched as he wrestled with the man. Then the man said, 'Let me go, for it is daybreak.'

But Jacob replied, 'I will not let you go unless you bless me.'

The man asked him, 'What is your name?'

'Jacob,' he answered.

Then the man said, 'Your name will no longer be Jacob, but Israel, because you have struggled with God and with humans and have overcome.'

Jacob said, 'Please tell me your name.'

But he replied, 'Why do you ask my name?' Then he blessed him there.

So Jacob called the place Peniel, saying, 'It is because I saw God face to face, and yet my life was spared.'

I remember reading about a couple who had been married for over 80 years—a British record at the time. The elderly pair were asked what they believed the secret of their marriage was. The husband quickly answered that the secret simply consisted of two words: 'Yes, dear'! There may well be some amount of truth in his answer, but our reading today teaches us something else about successful relationships, and in particular about our relationship with God. The man with whom Jacob found himself struggling was no ordinary person, but a representation of God. Even the name given to Jacob that night, Israel, means 'he who struggles with God'. Interestingly, the fact that Jacob struggles both with God and with his fellow humans is not necessarily seen by God as a bad thing. The blessing he gives to Jacob seems to imply that struggles are a good and positive thing, as is the fact that we can overcome such tussles.

All our relationships involve some amount of struggling with each other. We wrestle with issues, questions or viewpoints which we hold dear or to which we object. As long as we can reach a resolution, these struggles are an important and healthy part of our relationships. In the Jacob story, the resolution comes at daybreak, and it often seems to us that the sun is breaking through the darkness when our struggles conclude.

So this story affirms to us that it is natural and right to struggle with God. It is far more dangerous to refuse to struggle, and to keep our pain, suffering, issues and problems locked inside a dark safe in our soul. As the theologian Dietrich Bonhoeffer put it: 'In the darkness of the unexpressed, evil poisons the whole being of a person.' If we have something on our mind, we must take it to God and express it.

Recently, I read a short story by the German writer Ingo Schulze, entitled 'Cell Phone'. In it he describes an abandoned car on a street in Berlin, which has been there for weeks. Each day, he would look out of his window at that car. At first, rubbish started collecting round it and the flyers wedged under the wipers began to yellow. Then, one morning, he noticed a wheel had gone missing. Two days later, the registration plates were gone, along with the other three wheels. Next, a rock was thrown through the window.

Eventually, as he was walking home one evening, he was shocked to find the car had been set alight and was in flames. The moral of the tale, writes Schulze, is that 'you shouldn't let junk even start to collect'.

We must not be afraid to carry our junk to God. We can take our questions, issues and problems to him, and struggle through them with him. Our relationship with God has similarities to our human relationships. Both include rosy, happy moments of fun and joy, but they also include struggling and wrestling. Thrashing out those struggles is often what keeps a relationship flourishing. As Woody Allen perceptively observed in his film Annie Hall (1977), 'A relationship, I think, is like a shark; it has to constantly move forward or it dies.' Unlike our human relationships, though, God will never let us down because his love for us is unchanging and eternal. If we allow ourselves to be challenged by God, we will find that our relationship with him is reinvigorated and keeps moving forward.

## Reflection

*Our struggle with God may involve us going to fellow Christians for support and guidance—God can, after all, speak and work through other people. Alternatively, we can involve God directly. 'Take it to the Lord in prayer,' as Joseph M. Scriven's hymn 'What a friend we have in Jesus' (1855) asserts. Talk to Christ about your struggles, your worries and your doubts. Don't be afraid to cry and shout or to smile and laugh. Allow him to reassure you and to show you his love. After your prayer, if you feel the need, you could phone a good friend for a chat.*

# 5–6 January

# Putting our hand in his hand

When I used to tell people I was training for ordination, I'd very often have the same reaction. 'Oh poor you,' they'd say. 'You'll have to work over Christmas!' Like many other people in various occupations, I do, indeed, have to work over the festive period. Before you get the hankies and violins out for me, let me tell you that this is certainly not the worst job I've had over Christmas. When I was 16 years old, I worked at a burger bar. That restaurant had an annoying mascot called Mr Wimpy, who dressed as a Beefeater from the Tower of London. As I was the youngest worker there, I was the poor soul who had to dress up as Mr Wimpy for the children's Christmas parties. I'd be wearing a big, round costume, in which I would be looking through a hole in Mr Wimpy's hat, with his eyes at the level of my chest and his mouth down by my legs. This, sadly, left his large nose in a very unfortunate place. In other words, every time a child hit Mr Wimpy's nose, which they did very often, let's just say it made my eyes water! 'What's a bit of humiliation, if it'll bring more money in?' said our store manager when I complained.

Jesus also suffered humiliation at Christmas, but that humiliation was nothing to do with money or materialism. Here was our Lord and Saviour, the prince of peace, being born to a teenage girl – and not in a wonderful palace or in a private hospital, but in a humble stable, among the dirt and the animals. As Philip Yancey wrote, 'The God who roared, who could order armies and empires about like pawns on a chessboard, this God emerged in Palestine as a baby who could not speak or eat solid food or control his bladder, who depended on a teenager for shelter, food and love.' Jesus' humiliation continued throughout his life, from his birth in a stable to his crucifixion at Calvary. The Mel Gibson-directed film *The Passion of the Christ*, which packed out cinemas on its release in 2004, shows the extent of the violence and hatred shown towards Jesus at the end of his earthly life. Whatever we are going through, we can be reassured that the incarnation means that God knows what it is to be humiliated. He understands what suffering is and he stands alongside us when we are going through difficult times.

# Trusting him

**Matthew 14:22–33**

Immediately Jesus made the disciples get into the boat and go on ahead of him to the other side, while he dismissed the crowd. After he had dismissed them, he went up on a mountainside by himself to pray. Later that night, he was there alone, and the boat was already a considerable distance from land, buffeted by the waves because the wind was against it.

Shortly before dawn Jesus went out to them, walking on the lake. When the disciples saw him walking on the lake, they were terrified. 'It's a ghost,' they said, and cried out in fear.

But Jesus immediately said to them: 'Take courage! It is I. Don't be afraid.'

'Lord, if it's you,' Peter replied, 'tell me to come to you on the water.'

'Come,' he said.

Then Peter got down out of the boat, walked on the water and came towards Jesus. But when he saw the wind, he was afraid and, beginning to sink, cried out, 'Lord, save me!'

Immediately Jesus reached out his hand and caught him. 'You of little faith,' he said, 'why did you doubt?'

And when they climbed into the boat, the wind died down. Then those who were in the boat worshiped him, saying, 'Truly you are the Son of God.'

About six years ago I visited Australia with work, but rather than concentrating on the job at hand, I decided to live the life of an action man. Instead of surfing at Bondi Beach or jet skiing off Botany Bay, though, I decided to travel up to the Snowy Mountains to try my hand at snowboarding and skiing. After a day on the nursery slopes with children whizzing past me, I decided it was time for the adult slope. I rode the ski-lift to the top, then took a deep breath and enthusiastically pushed myself off. What a thrill that was… for the first five seconds anyway. I remember shouting, 'Woo hoo, I'm James Bond!' before it dawned on me that I was travelling at up to 40 mph down the side of the highest mountain in Australia. I started to panic, looking at my skis to check my feet were in the correct position. Looking at my feet was certainly not a wise move. I don't actually remember much from then on, apart from desperately trying not to choke on mouthfuls of snow. Nothing was there to stop me, and I tumbled down the mountain for what seemed like a lifetime. I ended up badly straining my Achilles tendon, which meant I had to suffer the humiliation of wearing slippers in work for a whole year!

Our reading today has numerous similarities with my fall Down Under. Peter was certainly full of enthusiasm and faith when he leapt off the boat to walk across to Jesus. The Gospels describe Peter as the keen disciple, always the first to volunteer to do or say things. He reminds me a bit of the donkey in the *Shrek* films, always shouting, 'Pick me, pick me!' When Peter first left the boat, he was completely focused on Jesus and everything was going well. Then he probably looked around at the weather conditions and began to realise the amazing thing he was doing. Doubt and panic took over, and his fall was inevitable. Unlike my skiing catastrophe, however, there *was* someone there to catch Peter when he fell.

This story teaches us to keep focused on Jesus and on our faith, no matter how hard life seems to get. It also reassures us that it is only natural that we will, occasionally, be attacked by panic and doubt. Panic and doubt are part and parcel of life, as are slipping and falling. But we must have faith that when we fall, spiritually or emotionally, we only have to call out, as Peter did, and God will be there to catch us. On the BBC's *Breakfast* recently, there was an interview with one of the victims of the 7/7 London bomb blasts. This man had been in one of the tube carriages that was blown up. He described coming round from the blast, looking down at his mangled legs and immediately knowing that his life would never be the same again. 'I knew right away I was going to lose my right leg,' he recalled, 'but I kept telling myself to focus on God and not to panic; and, years later, I still wake up every day and tell myself the same thing—I should focus on God and not panic.' In such tragic circumstances he really was living out the lesson of our reading today.

## Reflection

*We all go through times of fear and doubt in our lives. Some of us face these on a daily basis. Spend some time in silence to clear your mind, then slowly repeat these inspiring words to yourself: 'Help me not to panic, Lord, and help me to focus on you.' Now take these words out into today, and into the next few days, to wherever you are going and whatever you are doing.*

# Peace in our hearts

### Matthew 6:25–34

'I tell you, do not worry about your life, what you will eat or drink; or about your body, what you will wear. Is not life more than food, and the body more than clothes? Look at the birds of the air; they do not sow or reap or store away in barns, and yet your heavenly Father feeds them. Are you not much more valuable than they? Can any one of you by worrying add a single hour to your life?

'And why do you worry about clothes? See how the flowers of the field grow. They do not labour or spin. Yet I tell you that not even Solomon in all his splendour was dressed like one of these. If that is how God clothes the grass of the field, which is here today and tomorrow is thrown into the fire, will he not much more clothe you—you of little faith? So do not worry, saying, "What shall we eat?" or "What shall we drink?" or "What shall we wear?" For the pagans run after all these things, and your heavenly Father knows that you need them. But seek first his kingdom and his righteousness, and all these things will be given to you as well. Therefore do not worry about tomorrow, for tomorrow will worry about itself. Each day has enough trouble of its own.'

### Philippians 4:4–7

Rejoice in the Lord always. I will say it again: rejoice! Let your gentleness be evident to all. The Lord is near. Do not be anxious about anything, but in every situation, by prayer and petition, with thanksgiving, present your requests to God. And the peace of God, which transcends all understanding, will guard your hearts and your minds in Christ Jesus.

People who meet me often comment that I seem cool, calm and collected, as if I can take everything in my stride. They shouldn't be fooled by appearances! In fact, I am a born worrier, with my mind programmed to fret about anything and everything. I remember being nine years old and being sent to the headmaster's office for causing an outbreak of panic in the school. I'd dragged a box of books from the library into the playground, stood on it, and, like some Old Testament prophet of doom, persuaded my school friends that the Falklands War would lead to a nuclear third world war and we'd be lucky if we even made it to secondary school. The apocalypse didn't happen, but I did get two weeks' detention!

Unfortunately, I took my propensity to worry with me into my adult life. I'd worry about work, about upsetting people, about money and about health. At one point I even started worrying that I hadn't got anything to worry about! Today's readings give us a wonderful picture of freedom from anxiety. In the Philippians passage, Paul encourages us to allow Christ to calm our worries and bring peace to our hearts and minds. In the Matthew passage, Christ points to the natural world to inspire us to turn away from the distinctly human propensity to worry.

In the Welsh language, we have two words for peace— *heddwch* and *tangnefedd*. On the one hand, *heddwch* is to be found on the outside of us—a peace between people or between nations. This is what most of us believe the

Christmas angels proclaimed with their vision of 'peace on earth'. *Tangnefedd*, on the other hand, is internal and eternal—a peace which reaches the depths of our souls. The incarnation may well bring the hope of *heddwch* on earth, but it can guarantee us *tangnefedd* inside, even when there is no peace outside of us. After all, changing the outside circumstances will not necessarily stop us worrying. The most this can offer is a temporary fix. We might worry about money, but even if we suddenly win the lottery, we'll soon find something else to worry about! It's only by changing the circumstances inside of us, and so changing the way we view our everyday challenges, that we begin to realise that most of what we worry about is not actually important.

Whatever the world might want us to believe, fame and recognition don't matter, and neither does popularity, wealth, success or outward appearance. Such a realisation can be *so* liberating, and can help to ease our worries, not that worry is something we can get rid of immediately. If we have an inclination towards worry or fear, as many of us do, then there is no quick fix. But, as someone who is on this journey away from worry, I know that if we put our hand in his hand, Christ can release our minds from being incarcerated by fear, and can lead us towards *tangnefedd*—the peace of God, which passes all understanding.

## Reflection
*The incarnation reassures us that God knows what it is like to have the cares of the world on our shoulders, and he truly wants us to offload those cares on to him. As we come to the end of our journey, pause to give thanks for the gift of the incarnation, and ask God to help you work on replacing your worries with* tangnefedd *in both your mind and your heart.*

# Using this book with a group

While this book has principally been written for individuals, it can also be used effectively in a small-group setting. Members are advised to follow individually the readings and reflections each day, then come together each week to share and discuss their thoughts and contemplations. To stimulate group discussion, the questions below are based on each week's readings. There are also weekly suggestions for concluding times of prayer.

## 1–7 December: The Word made flesh
1. How has Christ come through into your everyday life in the past few weeks? Share with the group those moments when Christ was revealing himself in your journey.
2. Discuss together how you picture Jesus. How do the different pictures of Jesus vary in appearance or character? What can you learn from other people's pictures?
3. Consider images that you have seen of Jesus—perhaps in paintings or in films. Share them with each other and discuss their similarities and differences.
4. How busy are the next few weeks going to be for you? Discuss your plans for Christmas, detailing what you are most looking forward to and also your concerns about the festive season.

**For prayer**

Pray that we will recognise God's presence in the upcoming celebrations—in the people we will see, in the places we will visit, in the moments of joy or fun and in the instances of seriousness or silence. However busy we are going to be and however challenging the situations we may face, we ask God to reveal himself to us this Christmas.

# 8–14 December: Christ in our neighbour

1. Take some time to get to know each other further. Each of you could share two interesting facts about yourself that others in the group might not know. The more time we take to get to know someone, the more we can recognise our shared humanity and see Christ in each other.
2. How difficult is it to wear 'Christ-tinted spectacles' and therefore to see Jesus in the people we meet? Why do you think many of us find this challenging?
3. How important do you think servanthood should be in our faith? What kind of little things can we do in our day-to-day lives to follow Jesus' example?
4. Consider some good deeds and actions that we could do over the Christmas period. Are there some things that we could all decide to commit to doing over the next few weeks?

**For prayer**

Pray that God helps us recognise Christ in the 'other', not just in our friends and family and not just in Christians, but in *all* people that we come across. Ask God to strengthen us to take opportunities over Christmas to serve others as if we were serving Christ himself.

# 15–21 December: Christ in the natural world

1. What part of the natural world do you connect with most frequently? What is it about nature that inspires you or lifts your heart?
2. Many of us have at least one place in the world we would love to visit or revisit, often because of the breathtaking scenery. Where would you choose to go? Explain to the group why you have chosen this particular place.
3. Most if not all of us enjoy the beauty of nature in one form or another. However, even some Christians do not relate this to the incarnational presence of Jesus. How easy is it for us to recognise Christ in the natural world?
4. In what ways can we carry out the biblical imperative to look after our environment? What steps can we take over Christmas to ensure our celebrations damage the environment as little as possible?

**For prayer**

Pray that we would allow the natural world to teach us something about our faith. Ask God to allow nature to inspire our beliefs, as we recognise Christ in the midst of it.

# 22–28 December: Christ in our lives

1. How difficult is it to remember the real meaning of Christmas over the festive season? What can we do, and what safeguards can we put in place, to ensure that Christ does not get forgotten in our celebrations?
2. How can we ensure that we find time and space for God over the Christmas period? Discuss how each of you are going to take moments to slow down the pace of the Christmas rush and open your eyes to God's presence.

3. In which of the following do you find that Christ comes to you most naturally and frequently—laughter, music, memories, food, film or friends? Give examples of when they have inspired you and brought you hope.
4. Take turns to share a happy memory of a past Christmas. When was it? Who did you share it with? What happened? In what way do you think Christ was present at that Christmas?

**For prayer**

Pray that God gives us opportunities for time and space to recognise his Son in the celebrations over Christmas. Ask that he helps us to lay aside any worries and concerns about the hectic nature of the festive season and focus on the real meaning of the incarnation.

# 29 December–4 January: Being Christ in the world

1. Discuss your God-given talents and gifts with each other. What does each of you have to offer for God's glory in this world? Remember that these need not be big and obvious talents, but could be smaller and more subtle ones that bring a little bit of light into other people's lives.
2. Why do you think it is difficult for us to think of ourselves as saintly? Share examples of when you have seen or experienced 'saintly actions' being carried out. How can we put 'saintly actions' into our own lives?
3. How different is the way the contemporary world views talent and fame compared with the way Christ lived? How can we ensure that we follow Christ's example, not buying into the prevalent attitudes about what makes people important and worthwhile?

4. Discuss examples of times when you felt God calling and leading you. As we look ahead to the New Year, what practical steps of love and compassion do you believe God is calling you to carry out in the coming months?

**For prayer**
Pray for those who are going back to work or their normal routine after the festive season. Ask God to provide opportunities for us to use our gifts and talents for his praise and glory.

## 5–6 January: Putting our hand in his hand
1. How difficult is it to trust God when we are going through a time of darkness? Discuss moments when you have trusted God through a period of pain or suffering.
2. Were there moments over the Christmas period where busyness, stress and worry seemed too much to cope with? Was God able to bring calm, peace or reassurance to your situation?
3. Share with each other the ups and downs of your Christmas. Where in particular did you find that the light of Christ touched your lives? What did you find challenging about the festive season this year?
4. What are the most helpful insights that you have gained from the group discussions over the past few weeks?

**For prayer**
Pray for the light of Christ to shine where there is pain and suffering in our lives, and pray for peace and healing for any past suffering that still has a hold on us. Ask for God's blessing on the year ahead, and ask that he helps us to trust him in any difficulties or challenges we face on our journeys.

# Bibliography

Many of the quotations I have used in this book have been collected over many years from films, books, newspapers, music lyrics, reliable internet sources and television programmes. However, to give readers the opportunity to explore topics further, I include here a bibliography of the principal texts that have been quoted.

*The Green Bible: A Priceless Message That Doesn't Cost the Earth* (Collins, 2008)

Mitch Albom, *Tuesdays with Morrie: An Old Man, a Young Man and Life's Greatest Lesson* (Time Warner, 2006)

Karen Armstrong, *Twelve Steps to a Compassionate Life* (Bodley Head, 2011)

Augustine, *Confessions* (Penguin, 1961)

William Blake, *The Complete Poems* (Penguin, 1977)

Dietrich Bonhoeffer, *Life Together* (SCM, 1992)

Dietrich Bonhoeffer, *The Cost of Discipleship* (SCM, 2001)

Elizabeth Barrett Browning, *Aurora Leigh and Other Poems* (Penguin, 1995)

Geoffrey Chaucer, *The Canterbury Tales* (Penguin, 2003)

Charles Dickens, *A Christmas Carol* (Penguin, 2008)

Richard J. Foster and James Bryan Smith (ed.), *Devotional Classics: Selected Readings for the Individual and Groups* (Hodder and Stoughton, 2003)

Gerard Manley Hopkins, *Poems and Prose* (Penguin, 1985)

Trystan Owain Hughes, *Finding Hope and Meaning in Suffering* (SPCK, 2010)

Trystan Owain Hughes, *The Compassion Quest* (SPCK, 2013)

Mark Kermode, *The Good, the Bad and the Multiplex: What's Wrong with Modern Movies?* (Random House, 2012)

Martin Luther King Jr., *I Have a Dream: Writings and Speeches that Changed the World* (HarperCollins, 1992)

Karl-Josef Kuschel, *Laughter: A Theological Reflection* (SCM, 1994)

C. S. Lewis, *The Magician's Nephew* (HarperCollins, 1997)

Alister McGrath, *Christian Theology: An Introduction* (Blackwell, 2001)

Brennan Manning, *The Ragamuffin Gospel* (Authentic, 2009)

Michael Mayne, *The Enduring Melody* (DLT, 2007)

Thomas Merton, *The Intimate Merton: Thomas Merton's Life from His Journals* (Lion, 2006)

Thomas Merton, *Thomas Merton: Essential Writings* (Orbis, 2000)

Arthur Miller, *Death of a Salesman* (Penguin, 2000)

Anaïs Nin, *The Seduction of the Minotaur* (Penguin, 1993)

Kathleen Norris, Foreword in Beverley R. Gaventa and Cynthia Rigby (ed.), *Blessed One: Protestant Perspectives on Mary* (Westminster John Knox, 2002)

Ingo Schulze, 'Cell Phone', in Nadine Gordimer (ed.), *Telling Tales* (Bloomsbury, 2004)

E.F. Schumacher, *A Guide for the Perplexed* (Vintage, 1995)

Albert Schweitzer, *Albert Schweitzer: Essential Writings* (Orbis, 2005)

Dorothee Soelle, *Dorothee Soelle: Essential Writings* (Orbis, 2006)

Henry David Thoreau, *Walden; or Life in the Woods* (Dover, 1995)

Desmond Tutu, *God Has a Dream: A Vision of Hope for Our Time* (Rider, 2004)

Henry Vaughan, *The Complete Poems* (Penguin, 1976)

Rick Warren, *The Purpose Driven Life: What on Earth am I here for?* (Zondervan, 2002)

Philip Yancey, *What's So Amazing about Grace?* (Zondervan, 2002)

Philip Yancey, *The Jesus I Never Knew* (Zondervan, 2002)

# Enjoyed
## this book?

**Write a review**—we'd love to hear what you think.
Email: reviews@brf.org.uk

**Keep up to date**—receive details of our new books as they happen.
Sign up for email news and select your interest groups at:
www.brfonline.org.uk/findoutmore/

### Follow us on Twitter @brfonline

**By post**—to receive new title information by post (UK only), complete
the form below and post to: BRF Mailing Lists, 15 The Chambers, Vineyard,
Abingdon, Oxfordshire, OX14 3FE

| **Your Details** |
| --- |
| Name |
| Address |
| Town/City      Post Code |
| Email |

| **Your Interest Groups** ('Please tick as appropriate) |
| --- |
| ☐ Advent/Lent     ☐ Messy Church |
| ☐ Bible Reading & Study     ☐ Pastoral |
| ☐ Children's Books     ☐ Prayer & Spirituality |
| ☐ Discipleship     ☐ Resources for Children's Church |
| ☐ Leadership     ☐ Resources for Schools |

### Support your local bookshop
Ask about their new title information schemes.